ROLVENDEN SCHOOL

a history

Ed Adams

CANTERLEY
PUBLISHING

Published by Canterley Publishing
www.canterley.co.uk
info@canterley.co.uk

Printed in the United Kingdom.

ISBN-13: 978-1-9164981-7-4

First published 2021.

The production of this book would not have been possible without the support of the people of Rolvenden, who have responded to the project with much kindness. I am particularly grateful to the following contacts, both local and global, who helped me in various ways:

Janet Adams, Olive and Peter Austen, Mark Barrow, Peter Brown, Joanna Bryan, Judy Burvill, Maralyn Button, Sue Clout, Cathy and Maurice Dalton, John Drywood, Sue and Dick Dyer, Jack Gillett, Jane Grunstein, Sue Hatt, Ken Hayesmore, Teresa Haywood, John Hook, Ellen Jones, Michael Lester and Janet Gorham Lester, Steve Monk, Gary and Jacky Morris, Yvonne Osborne, John and Anita Rivers, Barbara Scott, Simon Spelling, Tim Spelling, Esme Thomas, Tony Vening, Judy Vinson and Lynda Watts.

Time and opportunity did not permit me to contact several others whose details had been given to me, but I thank them too for their willingness to help.

For access to their historic records relating to Rolvenden and its school, I thank the staff of the Kent History and Library Centre, Ashford and Tenterden Gateways, The National Archives, Lambeth Palace Library and the Church of England Record Centre.

I also owe a debt to previous researchers: the work of Harold Bowen, Reg Spelling, John Drywood and Jackie King frequently came to my aid. Mr Spelling noted in 1970 that he wished to research and write the history of the school himself, and sought out much material from surviving relatives of the early headmasters. The project eventually grew into his *Rolvenden Reflections*, but I am particularly glad to be able to reproduce some of the fruits of his research here. Mr Drywood used this, and also undertook further valuable research himself, for the 150th anniversary celebrations in 1987. But of the above-named I particularly wish to thank Jackie, whose assistance has been both critical to the project and freely and cheerfully given. With the recent passing of several of its contributors, her *Rolvenden Recollections* is becoming an invaluable primary source for the village's history. Thank you, Jackie.

These books cannot be produced without the co-operation of the school, and Nick Leggat has been most supportive and kind, despite the demanding nature of his role and the uniquely difficult circumstances of 2020-1. Sandy Hughes and Emma Catt have also rendered much practical assistance in accessing the archives, for which I am very grateful. Frances Clifford and Nikki Payne have been unfailing in their generosity, and it is a pleasure to support the Friends of Rolvenden School in return. Lastly, Sarah O'Neill first approved this project with great kindness and enthusiasm just before ill health compelled her to retire in 2019. I regret very much that she was unable to see the finished result.

While I have tried to give due representation to as many as possible who have been connected with the school throughout its history, the nature of staffing in more recent years – as well as certain gaps in the documentation available to me – means that those in the modern era cannot be given as much coverage as those in past times. Neither do I feel it right or fair to comment as fully on those currently associated with the school as I have done with those from a bygone era. If anyone feels that their contribution has been ignored or underplayed in consequence, I hope they will take this by way of an explanation.

Finally, I offer my most heartfelt thanks to my wife Frances, and my daughter Emily, who teaches me new things every day.

Chapter 1

THE FREE SCHOOL

1707-1837

DURING THE MIDDLE AGES, the only schools in existence were in the centres of government or religion, and catering to those boys destined for the clergy. In its isolated position near the Kent-Sussex border, Rolvenden was some distance from any of these. But by the sixteenth century a few further opportunities for education had appeared, when several 'free schools,' later converted to 'grammar schools,' were founded: at Cranbrook in 1518; Tenterden by 1521 (and perhaps as early as 1512); Biddenden in 1566; Sutton Valence in 1576.

Rolvenden did not have an established 'free school' in this era, but evidence suggests there was an arrangement whereby a schoolmaster was appointed to the parish. It would have been of an *ad hoc* nature; nonetheless, he required a licence to teach from the Archdeacon, who needed to be satisfied that the applicant was of the correct character. His pupils would probably not have numbered more than ten or so, and the appointments did not usually last very long. A licence to teach in Rolvenden was first issued in 1577 to a John Norden. 1582 saw the appointment of John Fright, who may have taught pupils from neighbouring Wittersham at the same time. He was replaced the following year by a William Atkinson, but the new man appears to have lasted only two more years. Giles Fanstone applied for a licence in 1585 but he was perhaps unsuitable as his record is marked with *non emanavit* – 'not issued.' A schoolmaster named Henry Rogers could have been present in the village by 1600, as his son was baptised in Rolvenden that year with his father's occupation given in the register; though the only Henry Rogers with a licence on record was at Marden in 1593. Schooling may have fallen into abeyance for a few years, or perhaps been taken on by the vicar, as the next licence is to a William Turner in 1617. Of these six named men, only John Norden held an MA: the rest were *literates* – that is, they held no university degree.

By the time of Turner's mastership at Rolvenden a 'free school' had been established semi-locally, at Benenden, by the will of Edmund Gibbon. The Gybbon family had been present in Rolvenden since at least 1326, and earned their fortune through the manufacture of broadcloth. In the reign of Henry VIII a Robert Gybbon bought the estate of Hole and had two sons: John and Jarvis, and very broadly, John's descendants remained in Rolvenden while those of Jarvis established themselves in Benenden. (The spelling of their surname is interchangeable, but – equally broadly – Rolvenden's line preferred 'Gybbon' whereas Benenden's tended to favour 'Gibbon.') It was Jarvis's son Edmund who founded the 'free school' at Benenden by his 1608 will, and a purpose-built building was constructed the following year which still stands at the north end of the village green. Like the ancient free schools of Tenterden and Biddenden, its endowment was eventually diverted into a National School (of which more later) and then a primary school, and the building was used for various purposes by Benenden's village school until very recently.

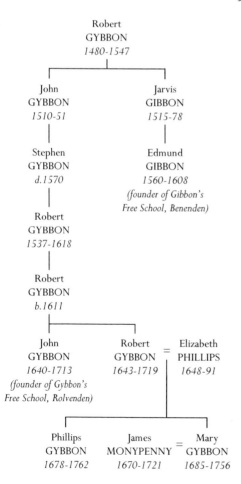

The Rolvenden line of Gybbons continued at Hole. After several more generations we arrive at Colonel Robert Gybbon, a prominent Parliamentarian during the Civil War and personal · friend of Oliver Cromwell. His loyalty was rewarded by his appointment as Governor of Jersey, a plum post which Gybbon seems to have turned to his great advantage. Contemporary accounts denounce him as a self-serving bully and autocrat who imposed unworkable laws on the islanders and laid out unjust and unlawful punishments to those who displeased him. Such were the complaints against him that he was replaced as

Governor and a formal enquiry into his conduct began, but this lost momentum on the death of Cromwell in 1658 and was never pursued. On the Restoration of Charles II in 1660 Gybbon greeted the new king at Dover and was obsequious enough to receive a pardon, and the estate of Hole was restored to him.

A few years later bubonic plague arrived in the village, and the population moved one mile down the road to the hamlet known as the

The original 1609 building of the Gibbons Free School, Benenden.

'Lain,' and – according to local legend – burned the houses they left behind to help stop the spread of the disease. This is why Rolvenden today is a parish of two halves: the Streyte, which is the site of the original village on the old Canterbury-Hastings road, and the Layne – larger than a hamlet but too small for a village in its own right. At about the same time Rolvenden enjoyed a tangential connection to the history of education, when in 1662 the Hoadly family moved to the village from Edinburgh. The following year their son Samuel began to teach at Cranbrook's grammar school, and so started a career that culminated in the writing of a textbook, the *Natural Method of Teaching*. This was a revolutionary text, combining Latin and English grammar in such a way as to become the most successful school manual of the time, and remained in print for over a century. It is very possible that Rolvenden's early pupils were to benefit from this writer's influence.

Of Colonel Robert's eldest son John Gybbon, little is known. He was probably born in Staplehurst in 1635 – there is a baptism record there which matches, and he remembered that place in his will. He was later married to Mary, though her lineage is obscure. He appears to have had no surviving children, so wasn't afforded a magnificent memorial of the type given to his younger brother Robert that stands in the nave of St Mary's, Rolvenden. He held the commission of Major in the militia, and for some portion of his career conducted business in the Charterhouse at Middlesex.

What is clear is that in June 1695 he bought three Exchequer annuities that each paid him £14 per year 'out of the Excise of Beer, Ale and other liquors for 96 years.' When he made his will twelve years later, on 20th November 1707, these annuities were bequeathed to his wife. On her death, they would then pass to his nephew Phillips and then to his niece Mary – both children of John's brother Robert. Then – crucially – on Mary's death, they would be given over to several named gentlemen to hold in trust. These men, largely from the Kadwell, Burden and Chittenden families, were either in-laws or business associates of the Gybbons.

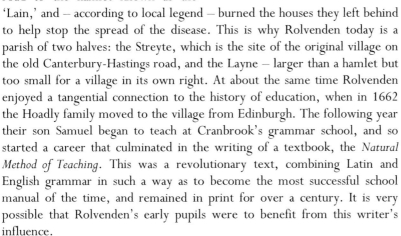

John Gybbon's trust was to provide for:

> the Churchwardens and overseers of the Poor for the time being of the Parish of Rolvenden... to be expended by them for the Schooling and educating [of] the Boys in reading, writing and casting accounts, and in teaching the Girls to read, knit and spin well both linen and woollen...

Any yearly revenue left over after the school and clothing expenses was to be put towards apprenticing school leavers in their chosen trade. In addition, a separate sum was to be put aside for the distribution of clothing to the parish poor each October.

The chain of bequests began on John's death in 1713 and the annuities found their way to his nephew Phillips Gybbon, who by then was the Whig Member of Parliament for Rye. His sister Mary had predeceased him by the time of his death on 11th March 1762, so the money went straight to the trustees – who, as the original named persons were also dead, were now the churchwardens and overseers of the poor. On this date, therefore, was the founding of the Gybbons Educational Trust, and thus the beginning of a formally-endowed school at Rolvenden.

As Major Gybbon's original annuities had only a fixed lifespan, and Exchequer annuities on excise were no longer a consistent source of income in any case, the first step was to transfer them into something more reliable. A decree in Chancery allowed them to be converted into '9 per cent consolidated bank stock,' which would give a dependable annual dividend of £27 12s 9d. Gybbon had directed that the accounts of his trust be recorded by the churchwardens and overseers of the poor 'in a distinct book from their other rates, charges and payments.' This book, which begins on establishment of the trust in 1762, still exists and is held at the Kent History and Library Centre, Maidstone.

It reveals that there was no one master or mistress appointed to a permanent position at the school, but rather a series of positions filled on a temporary basis, probably calculated to a daily rate, and paid quarterly. So for 1764 (the first year for which full accounts are available) we find three teachers taking on the duty: Mary Burden (for £7 2s 8d), Frances Kadwell (for £4 11s 1d) and Elizabeth Bridger £3 4s 3d). Some idea of their hierarchy can perhaps be gleaned from their respective wages. That said, men were invariably paid more: the school's first male teacher, Joseph Bigg, appears in 1771 and for a full year's teaching was given £8 9s 5d, compared with Mary Burden's £5 15s – though this also suggests that her duty had lightened in the intervening years.

Joseph Bigg taught at Rolvenden for only five years, leaving in 1775, and both Mary Burden and Elizabeth Bridger left around the same time. Of the first cohort, Frances Kadwell was the most enduring, lasting until 1783. By then another male teacher, Francis Metcalf, had taught for seven years. He is the first staff member to be definitively tied to Rolvenden from first to last: he was born there around 1715, and after spells – perhaps teaching – at

Sevenoaks, Lydd, Westerham and Goudhurst, he returned to his birthplace after being widowed and taught until his death in 1784. Another local teacher was Mary Tapply, who began at the same time as Francis Metcalf but outlasted him to the tune of 16 years, leaving around the turn of the century. In between, teachers came and went after perhaps three, four or five years, many with resolutely parochial names that are still heard in the neighbourhood today: Mary Elphee; Elizabeth Iden, Hannah Britcher; Elizabeth Pike; Mrs Kennard; Mrs Witherden.

An idea of the curriculum offered at Rolvenden's burgeoning school can be gained both by reference to John Gybbons' will, and by comparing it to other similar schools locally. Unlike those at Benenden, Biddenden and Tenterden, Latin grammar was not offered, and it therefore did not develop into what we would term a 'grammar school.' Perhaps the closest parallels can be drawn with the charity school founded in High Halden by the 1725 will of James Tilden, and that established as the Wittersham Free School in 1820 by the vicar of that parish, Rev. William Cornwallis. In common with that of Gybbons, Tilden's will also directed that children be taught in 'reading English, writing and casting accounts,' and later testimony suggests that the standard text for learning to read was the New Testament. The Cornwallis school offered 'reading, writing and understanding the English language, and the first four rules of Arithmetic… no books but the Bible, Common Prayer, and such as are recommended by the Society for Promoting Christian Knowledge are to be used.' The application of such founding trusts tended to vary, but it is a fair assumption that Rolvenden's school would have been conducted along similar lines. As to funding, it was worked out that after necessary expenses and payments to the staff, enough would be left in the pot for 25 boys (usually, in such cases, termed 'foundation scholars') to receive their education free of charge. But the survival of the school would very much depend on those others subsidising the rest by paying 'school pence.'

When Francis Metcalf died in 1783 his replacement was the head of a family that would provide an unbroken line of teachers that was to last for the next century and a half. He was also the first obvious candidate for Rolvenden School's 'headmaster.' **Joseph Jenner** was born in Wittersham in 1747, and at the time of his appointment had already been resident in or around Rolvenden for about ten years. He had married Mary Dewhurst there in October 1773; in something of a hurry, one assumes, as the couple's daughter Mary arrived only seven months later. Some 25 years later, she was to teach at the school alongside her father. At least three further children were born to the Jenners: Joseph in 1776, Anne in 1777 and James in 1783.

It is unclear where the school was actually conducted during the eighteenth century: most likely in the respective teachers' houses, or perhaps in part of the church. But it is known that until 1801, there were in fact two schools; one at the Streyte and one at the Layne. A note records that the latter was closed on 12th October of that year, 'the income of the Charity appearing to be inadequate' to support it. Presumably Hannah Britcher was in charge of this school, as payments to her now ceased – and of course, her family name has a long association with the Layne. This left only father and daughter, Joseph and Mary Jenner, running one school at the Streyte together in straightened circumstances. Not helping the situation was a longstanding debt of a year's income that had been lent to help prop up the clothing fund in 1769, and had still not been paid back. The trustees now felt justified to call it in, though it took two years to balance the books again.

But better news was on the way, as in 1804 a purpose-built school was provided at what is now 36-46 High Street. The trustees' account book is silent on the issue of who paid for it: it was most likely the parish Committee (forerunner of the parish council), which would have consisted largely of the same people, and it was therefore funded through local taxes. And, as if to reaffirm the close correlation between poverty and education, it was sited adjacent to the village poor-house. Now divided into several properties, it is a long, red brick building with six casement windows over two storeys, and may well have included living quarters for the Jenner family as well as the two necessary schoolrooms. A drawing of its situation in the high street, produced perhaps some thirty years after its construction, reveals that it originally enjoyed two large arched mullion windows, criss-crossed with glazing bars.

James Oxley's sketch of Rolvenden's High Street, showing the 1804 school building (extreme right).

For three years the new school continued to be run exclusively by Joseph Jenner and his daughter, who married during this time and became Mary Landsell. His family continued to expand: in 1798 daughter Anne had married John Oxley, a native of Benenden variously described as a butcher or farmer, and the couple's son James arrived on the penultimate day of the

The old school building at 36-46 High Street today.

following year. Then, on 25ᵗʰ March 1807, Joseph died, aged 59. His death notice in the press described him as 'of the Free School, at Rolvenden' — the first time the parish school is known to have been referred to by this name. What began as a disparate and perhaps rather unsatisfactory collection of teachers and pupils had by now blossomed organically into a 'school,' run on modern lines with a master at its head, almost exactly a century after the will of its benefactor.

The day after his father's death, youngest son **James Jenner**, then 23 years old, married his bride Anne Cheeseman in her home village of Leigh, near Tonbridge. (News of his bereavement may have reached him there, or when the couple returned to Rolvenden.) Once the burial rites of Joseph Jenner had been completed at Rolvenden on 1ˢᵗ April the mastership of the school passed to James, and he worked alongside his sister until she gave way to Eliza Smith in 1810. The accounts suggest a short-lived boom in the number of pupils: from 1811 Ann Coveney was taken on, further supplemented by Sarah Russell in 1816. It was the first time the school had been able to afford four teachers in nearly two decades.

It also appears that, from 1817, they gained a fifth member of staff in the form of James Jenner's nephew James Oxley, the 17-year-old son of his sister Anne. Payments to Master Oxley do not appear in the trustees' accounts, so it is possible he was paid directly out of his uncle's salary — but it is certain from later testimony that he began his teaching career at Rolvenden at this time.

The boom, it appears, did not last. Almost from the moment of James Oxley's arrival the school was running at a loss. Each yearly school account recorded money out of pocket, while the clothing account enjoyed cash in hand. This situation reached its nadir in 1821, when the clothing account held a healthy £138 and the school was £26 in the red. While the overall balance of both accounts was on the right side of the line (and it always was) the trustees were able to prop up one with cash from the other, but it hid an uncomfortable truth: the school, seen as an entity on its own, could not pay its way. A twenty-year economy drive was undertaken, during which time James Jenner was the only staff member named on the accounts. He was not working alone – nephew James was also there, and it is unlikely that there was not at least one other – but his school was certainly running on a shoestring. Year-on-year, the deficit was very gradually reduced, but it would never be fully balanced again.

Clearly, the free education of only 25 boys was proving inadequate for a parish the size of Rolvenden, and not enough parents felt that their children's education was worth the payment – which would have been a considerable outlay for the poorest labourers with the most children. A solution had existed since 1811 with the foundation of the National Society for Promoting Religious Education, which offered grants to establish schools conducted strictly along Church of England principles, which would then offer a greatly subsidised education at a lower price. Tenterden was one of the first places to establish a 'National School,' converting its ancient grammar school trust for the purpose in 1812. But herein lay a problem as generally, non-conformists – Baptists, Wesleyans, Methodists and the like – refused to support such Anglican schools. The Weald of Kent had traditionally been a stronghold for such religious dissent, and Rolvenden had a particular notoriety in this area, with the Layne's connection to John Wesley and a celebrated magistrate's trial held in 1760, where several of Wesley's local followers were found guilty of an illegal religious gathering, and therefore a breach of the Conventicle Act.

Rev. John Hooper, vicar of Rolvenden 1833-54.

Although precise details are not known, it is quite obvious that in its earlier history there was a thread of non-conformism running through the Rolvenden Free School. The Bigg and Pike families were dissenters, and some members of each were defendants at the 1760 trial. It is more than likely that several of the Gybbons trustees were also non-conformists. This would help to explain why when Rolvenden's vicar Rev. John Hooper tried to persuade the trustees to divert their funds into the founding of a brand new National School towards the end of 1833, he was curtly informed that they 'were of the opinion that they would not be justified in applying their funds in any other manner than heretofore.' Hooper was undaunted, however, and got 'several respectable inhabitants' and at least one sympathetic trustee on his side. From the wealthier classes, he began to collect pledges of money and the annual subscriptions that would help to subsidise the cost of running the school. It was judged that, once the remaining trustees saw the local support and understood the advantages of the National system, they would be won over.

Plans were drawn up. The new school was to cater for 100 boys and 100 girls, with a separate classroom for each measuring 30 feet by 19 feet. It would open every weekday and, in a new initiative to satisfy the National Society, would also run Sunday classes as well, which each pupil would be required to attend. The estimated cost of the new school was £200; that is, £180 to build it, and a further £20 to equip it. At the end of February 1834, donors had pledged around £100. Five months later, the National Society promised another £105 to cover the rest of the project. There now seemed to be no stopping it.

From this confident start, though, things began to go wrong. Rev. Hooper originally intended the school to be built on a different site to where it stands today. Precisely where is unclear, but it was described as 'waste land attached to the churchyard,' which would have been owned by the church and thus would not have required a conveyance. For some reason this was deemed unsuitable and an alternative site found which was owned by the Dean and Chapter of Rochester. The land was willingly donated to the cause but, of course, a legal conveyance was now required which had not been budgeted for. The first trenches were dug but there then occurred a delay of three years before the foundations could be laid – again, the reason why is unknown, but it may be that extra expenses were identified, which were only covered by 'a handsome subscription offered me [Hooper] by the most influential individual in the parish.' During this time, it seems that something else happened to throw all the plans in the air, as Rev. Hooper explained to the National Society in April 1836:

> I am grieved to say the plan for establishing a weekly school for boys and girls has been for the present abandoned. It is proposed however to erect a building for a Sunday School for both sexes, and if appropriate a part of it to a weekly [school] for girls... I trust that, should I succeed in establishing the schools in question, it will not be long ere the formation of a weekly school for boys will follow.

The only likely explanation for this about-turn was that, during the long delay to the building work, the Gybbons trustees got cold feet, and either withdrew or withheld their support. The consequence would be that a pared-down Free School was to continue on weekdays for boys only, with the rest of the educational provision taken up by the new school. Luckily, though, wiser heads prevailed, and after a few months the original plan was once again back on track.

There were signs that the whole project suffered from a lack of diligence, or an excess of haste, or both. The building work was largely carried out by two firms: Thomas Harden and Oak Shoobridge, and it will be seen that, as was realised later, neither covered themselves in glory. Almost unbelievably, the architect's plans did not include chimneys to convey the smoke from fires out of the building, and these needed to be hurriedly added. Another unwelcome surprise stored up for later years was that the conveyance from the Dean and Chapter of Rochester was badly drafted and legally defective: it gave no indication as to what, besides religion, was to be taught, and no limits on the area from which the body of pupils might be drawn, which could have given rise to children from other parishes turning up at the school – if they paid, they could not legally be refused. And to put the tin hat on the whole thing, a stamp duty bill that was expected to be 35 shillings turned out to be nearer five pounds. The total cost of the school's establishment was £307, leaving the fund £93 in deficit before the doors opened to its first pupils.

At some point during 1835-6, James Jenner retired from the mastership of the Free School. The reason is unknown – he was only in his early fifties, and would live well into his 86th year, dying at Hammersmith in 1869. But whatever the reason, Jenner would take no further part in the running of either the old Free School or upcoming National School. Instead, he passed all his duties on to his nephew, who by now had twenty years' experience and had clearly earned his spurs. It was **James Oxley** who would take the education of Rolvenden into the Victorian era.

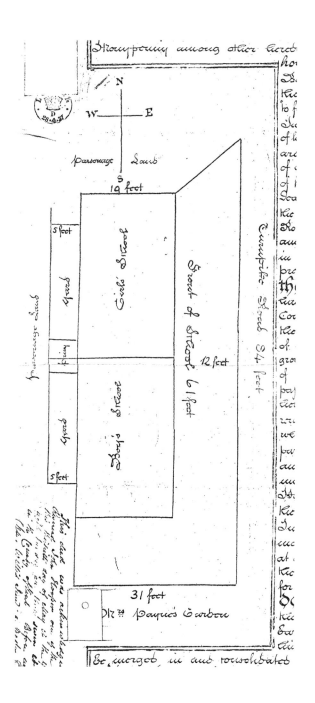

Chapter 2

A NATIONAL SCHOOL

1837-63

THE TRUST DEED that established Rolvenden National School was signed on 14th April 1837, and the building was certainly finished by that autumn as the final bills were being settled in October. It is therefore a fair assumption that children crossed the threshold of the new building for the first time that month, once hop-picking was over. Between the signing of the deed and the start of lessons, Great Britain and its Empire had gained a new queen: eighteen-year-old Victoria, who ascended to the throne on 20th June. Rolvenden National School thus saw itself coincide almost exactly with a new era in global history.

By this time James Oxley was Rolvenden's village *factotum*; that is, the go-to person for all educational and cultural matters. A later correspondent wrote:

> *He was collector of assessed and income-taxes, churchwardens' clerk and collector, assistant overseer, vestry clerk, clerk to the parochial charities, and organist at the parish church (and regularly present in that capacity every morning at the daily service).*

James Oxley's sketch of St Mary's church, 1834.

He was also the district enumerator for the three national censuses of 1841, 1851 and 1861, and is therefore owed a debt by genealogical researchers. But it was his artistic talent that was to be most remembered by the villagers. At least two of his sketches survive – one already seen, of the Free School in the High Street, and another of the view from his new school of the church across the road. Both are impressive in their delicacy and precision. As well as being the organist he conducted the choir of the parish church and, later, that of the church at Benenden as well. He also dabbled in musical composition, producing 'several chants and airs of considerable merit.'

With all this considered, it is difficult to conceive that James Oxley had any time left with which to run a school. Yet he not only taught perhaps three classes of boys aged seven to fourteen, who numbered around 60, he is also known to have taken on older pupils – including girls – in a private capacity. Now that the Free School in its own right had been wound up, the Gybbons trustees neatly reassigned their yearly income of £27 12s 9d to form the bulk of Mr Oxley's salary, which was topped up by further payments from the National School fund, and his private pupils, reaching an annual total in excess of £40.

His counterpart as the girls' mistress was Sarah Coveney, in her early sixties and on a salary of £35. Although less than Oxley's total earnings from the school, this was on the generous side for a female teacher at that time. It probably reflects both her age and experience, and the fact that from the start, Rolvenden bucked the national trend by educating slightly more girls than boys. A survey a few years later put the tally during the week as 59 boys and 65 girls. This was, however, somewhat fewer than the hoped-for totals of 100 boys and 100 girls which the school had been built to accommodate.

This shortfall was down to two reasons: one, the National School was not the only option for an education in Rolvenden. There were also a cluster of Dame Schools, invariably run by a widow or spinster who would open a room of her house and give rudimentary instruction to the youngest children for a few pence each week. This arrangement was entirely unregulated and amounted to little more than babysitting, but it was cheaper than the formal school and had been around for longer. One such example in the village was that run by Elizabeth Parnell, who also allowed her pupils to board for a supplement, and later on Sarah Care and Mary Austen also started similar ventures.

The second reason that numbers were smaller than expected was that attendance was still not compulsory, and would not be for another 30 years. In schools of this type, it was a universal struggle to convince the labouring parents, most of whom had not had any formal education of their own, of the merits of this new opportunity – still less to take their children out of the fields when they could be earning an income for the family. One way of winning hearts and minds was through Sunday schools: a condition of its alignment with the National Society was that the school be open for Anglican religious instruction for a few hours on the Sabbath, and Henry Elphee was taken on as the first Sunday school teacher from 1837. This met with some success, and within a few years the Sunday attendance matched or sometimes exceeded that of weekdays. But it did not win over the non-conformists, who made up a significant proportion of the labouring class, and whose children attended their own Sunday schools attached to their chapels.

The new National School received much-needed support from the landowning class, all of whom were invariably Anglican and thus much more sympathetic to the cause. An example was in June 1839, when Captain Thomas Gybbon-Monypenny, then Member of Parliament for Rye, held 'a Bazaar for the sale of fancy goods' at Hole Park in aid of the school funds. A newspaper of the time gushed that the Monypenny family…

> … *rendered every assistance in their power for the promotion of the undertaking. The grounds, which were gratuitously open on the occasion, were splendidly decorated, and throned with the fashionable families of the neighbourhood… In the lake was the Captain's pleasure boat gaily decked out, with the ensign and union jack flying. The tout ensemble presented a most delightful appearance. Upwards of £13 had been taken at four o'clock, for admission (at 1s. each) to the Bazaar.*

The report included a long list of the gentry who attended; but strikingly, the school's pupils and staff did not merit a single mention. This is indicative of the attitude to the early National Schools – they were laudably and often generously supported by the establishment, but at arm's length as a personal indulgence; and only with the object of keeping the books balanced, rather than conveying much of tangible benefit to the children.

An early portrait of James Oxley.

Mrs Coveney fell ill at about the time of this event and was unfit to work for around six months – she was only paid up to midsummer, and her position was put in jeopardy, with the post advertised in the press. Happily she recovered and remained at the school for at least another three years. In more good news, May 1840 saw the marriage of James Oxley to Mercy Richardson in the bride's home village of Benenden. The union was productive: both in terms of Mr Oxley's links with the neighbouring village, which flourished; and children, who appeared at more-or-less regular eighteen-month intervals over the next few years.

James Oxley is known to have been a keen cricketer – his name appears in the accounts of many Rolvenden matches played in the 1840s. It is quite possible that one of his pupils at both the old Free School and the new National School was Edgar Willsher of Little Halden Farm, and if so it is perhaps likely that this young man was encouraged in taking up the sport by his schoolmaster. If so, James Oxley is worthy of a footnote in the history of the game, for Willsher went on to play first-class cricket for Kent. He is credited with being the first player to promote overarm bowling, which was eventually made legal and replaced the older 'roundarm' style.

A new mistress was certainly in place by 1844 – unnamed, but probably Jane Johnston, in her early twenties and of Pix's Farm, whose name appears in a village directory listing of 1847. At the end of that same year, tragedy struck the Oxley household when Mercy Oxley died in childbirth on 21st December; her infant son Arthur lived for only a few months. Pointers to this sad and painful situation are found in the school accounts: Henry Elphee, the Sunday School teacher, had his pay suddenly doubled to £10 – probably to cover some of the duties of the grieving Mr Oxley.

Jane Johnston gave up her position as schoolmistress on becoming Mrs Frederick Chacksfield in March 1850 – or more likely, a little earlier, when the necessity to get married became clear; the couple's first child was born four months after the ceremony. Her replacement at the school was 40-year-old Elizabeth Fyles, originally from Hertfordshire, who had been widowed at the same time as Mr Oxley. She brought with her some of her five children, and at least two, Alice and Elizabeth, were promptly enrolled in the village school.

In March 1854 arrived one of Rolvenden's shortest-serving vicars, Rev. Henry Meeres, who would stay in the village for perhaps only eighteen months. He was a capable man with a particular interest in education, having spent two years as headmaster of the Cathedral Grammar School in Rochester. Yet at Rolvenden he stored up a sum of trouble by acting in a cavalier fashion with money matters. He was given around £21 – a considerable sum – by the retiring vicar Rev. Hooper to spend on the school. Meeres later claimed to have disposed of £10 in this way, though he kept no account of exactly how it was spent. The remaining £11 was apparently returned to Rev. Hooper because he had 'credited the school account with many subscriptions which he never received.' The nub of the latter issue was that the parents were taking advantage of Mr Oxley's good nature: they sent their children to school without paying the weekly fee, and were allowed to get into arrears which were quietly forgotten and never paid off.

Elizabeth Fyles departed at the end of 1855: while her son Henry remained in nearby Tenterden for some time, she moved to Yorkshire where she continued teaching, and died in 1868, aged 57. She was followed as mistress at the school by 24-year-old Emily Tuer, a native of Rolvenden who had most likely herself been taught by James Oxley, and who began her position on New Year's Day 1856. She was the daughter of Charles Tuer, a glazier and plumber for whom the new school had provided a constant trickle of work since its opening.

Another newcomer was Rev. John Rumsey, who as vicar would prove to be more lasting than his predecessor, remaining in Rolvenden for 29 years. Unlike many in his profession he was not a product of university but the publishing industry, though he maintained a strong interest in education, becoming the headmaster of Orsett School in Essex, where he was also the village curate. Very shortly after his arrival in Rolvenden, and a week after Emily Tuer's, a meeting was held 'to explain the state of the school and its affairs to the vicar and to request him to take the superintendence into his hands.' No more details are available, but it is clear from the tone of this note that there was some dissatisfaction in the air.

Rev. John Rumsey, vicar of Rolvenden 1855-84.

It was a few months later that the school received a Diocesan inspection – the earliest one of which any record survives – which was distinctly measured in its praise. Mr Oxley's top class of boys was 'very accomplished' with a 'fair knowledge of Scripture and of Catechism,' but their master was described as 'old school' and 'unused to modern modes of teaching.' Miss Tuer fared less well with the girls: 'the mistress appeared to be aware of their deficiency but not to know how to remedy it... writing on paper [is] very poor.' It was implied that the infants' textbooks were outdated, the wooden schoolroom floor unsuitable, and that help in the form of a monitor or pupil teacher – a recent school leaver in the first phase of training for a teaching career – was badly required. But there appeared no remedy for these problems while the accounts were unbalanced.

The new vicar was nothing if not proactive, and set about trying to sort the hole in the finances left by Rev. Meeres a few years earlier. For a long time his predecessor was unavailable – or refused – to attend a meeting to discuss the issue. Then when he suddenly became available in July 1858 one was called in great haste, to which Rumsey took exception, believing that there should have been at least a week's notice given for others to attend. The vicar also found himself at odds with his fellow school managers, Captains Tweedie and Weller, who decided for the sake of argument that the unknown sum spent on the school by Rev. Meeres in 1854 should be reckoned as £10. Rev. Rumsey wrote in the account book:

> *I opposed the decision as regards the £10 because it seemed impossible, after examining the accounts for 1854 and 1855 and also looking over all the other years and considering all possible ways of expenditure, that it could have been spent for any thing on behalf of the schools. I record this to justify myself to those who may hereafter take exception at the proceedings of the meeting.*

Rev. Rumsey was also determined to put a stop to the practice of children being allowed to attend without payment upfront. He gave Mr Oxley and Miss Tuer strict instructions not to accept such children into their classes, compiled a list of all those whose payments were in arrears, and then called on each family personally to collect the outstanding money. Unfortunately for the vicar, at every visit he was told where to go in no uncertain terms. But as a compromise, he offered to cancel any old debts if the children would, in future, pay on attendance or in advance.

Rev. John Riche Coombe, who was vicar of Tenterden until 1830 but lately living in retirement at Sparkeswood House, died in May 1855 and left £50 towards the school funds, as well as a further sum for the benefit of Rolvenden's poor. The legacy to the school was used to effect improvements to the building: a new brick floor replaced the substandard wooden one, and a porch for hats and coats, as well as a wall marking the boundary with the Hastings road, were both added. It was also during this time that the building of a schoolhouse for the master was first discussed. The reference to this is puzzling, as what later became known as School House is overwhelmingly likely to have already existed at this time. But it is quite possible that it came into the school managers' hands without them having to build a new one, and it would be in use as such within a few years.

Another inspection loomed in April 1860, and this time the praise was even more lukewarm and harder to find. On Mr Oxley's boys:

> *Writing and arithmetic are the points of success and there is a fair knowledge of scripture among the older children. But other attainments are deficient; and the lower classes though better organised than before are taught far too little.*

James Oxley, c.1854, with four of his children; (l-r) James, Edith, Albert and Ann.

And Miss Tuer's girls:

> The cleanliness and the needlework of the school deserve praise. The mistress is not untrained but insufficiently educated; and her methods of instruction are bad. Consequently both in reading, writing and arithmetic the girls are very backward and the religious knowledge of the first class is moderate, that of the second class next to nothing.

The key problem, as previously, was that Mr Oxley was the product of a bygone age of teaching. By the 1860s progress in educational methods had been such as to render the classroom environment rather different to that of Oxley's schooldays in the 1800s and the years of his training in the 1810s. And if Miss Tuer had herself been taught the same outdated methods by Oxley, that only compounded the problem. It would be as if a teacher trained in the 1950s took on a class in a school today: no-one would doubt their intelligence or ability, but they would be unlikely to satisfy either the requirements of a modern inspector, or the expectations of today's pupils.

None of this, however, appears to have dented the confidence in Mr Oxley and Miss Tuer displayed by the managers, the vicar, and the village at large. As if Oxley's workload were not heavy enough, in 1861 he and Rev. Rumsey started evening classes at the school on two nights each week. On payment of a penny for each session, around twenty young men of the labouring class were taught reading, writing and arithmetic in a welcome opportunity to supplement their childhood education – if indeed, one had been present at all. In the day school, 17-year-old John Harden was taken on as an assistant, in deference to the inspector's continued observation that one was urgently needed. The Sunday School continued under a succession of teachers: George Dawson gave way to Frederick Tapply in 1858; Thomas Burden in 1861; Fidge Russell two years later.

By this time the inspector had managed to find some progress in the right direction, as he wrote in July 1862:

> *The desks added to the school are a great improvement, and even another group would not be amiss. The books also are more suitable: but the reading is bad. There is an improvement in the orderly classification of the boys, and in their power of answering questions on religious subject. I should recommend that the assistant's chief attention be given to the two lower classes.*

> *The girls are improved in discipline and the first class are very fairly taught: the second class however follow them with too great an interval.*

Taking all things into account, by 1863 the provision of education in Rolvenden was assured. It was available widely, cheaply, and easily to those who wanted it, and the evidence shows that more and more were taking up the opportunity – nearly 200 pupils by this time. Despite never being to the total satisfaction of the education officials, James Oxley and Emily Tuer acquitted themselves well enough to retain the respect and confidence of the people of Rolvenden, for whom they worked tirelessly. So much so, that for their school duties, both enjoyed semi-frequent pay rises and, in 1863 Mr Oxley was even awarded a substantial bonus of £5 from the managers.

It was a fitting mark of esteem in what would turn out to be his last year of service. Before beginning the school day on the morning of Thursday 12th November, James Oxley suffered a sudden fit of paralysis and was confined to bed. Rev. Rumsey was hurriedly called, and attempted to give the patient Holy Communion, which he was unable to take. His condition deteriorated and he died just before noon the following day, Friday 13th November, aged 63.

In a display of the widespread affection in which James Oxley was held, his funeral six days later was attended by 400 mourners, with blinds and drapes drawn at every window of the village. Four church organists – of Ashford, Willesborough, Tenterden and Benenden – were pall-bearers, and the combined choirs of Rolvenden and Benenden led the congregation in the funeral rite that was entirely sung from beginning to end. Rev. Rumsey reflected shortly afterwards:

> *We have lost a laborious, kind, and gentle teacher; an accomplished and devout Church musician, and an upright, hard-working, public servant… He was literally worn out by hard work.*

Chapter 3

CHANGE AND CHALLENGE

1864-79

ON 18TH JANUARY 1864, **Francis William Parker**, a recent graduate of St Mark's College, Chelsea, travelled down to Rolvenden and presented himself for interview with the school managers. He was barely 20 years old, yet inspired such confidence that he was duly appointed as the school's next headmaster. Parker was born in the village of Barley, Hertfordshire, and became a pupil teacher at the village school there; aside from this, Rolvenden was his first teaching position in his own right. As it turned out, it would be his only one. He found Rolvenden not so different from Barley – both were rural settlements heavily dependent on agriculture, with a scattered population of farmers and labourers, and just a few examples of the landed gentry and members of the professional classes. If anything, perhaps, the rich were richer and the poor poorer, so while the school might be expected to receive greater support, its pupils faced a harder struggle.

As the managers must have hoped, from starting on 12th February Mr Parker threw himself into his role with youthful energy and vigour. We are fortunate that his log books, the daily journal he was required to keep, still exist and are kept at the school to this day. They give an invaluable insight into the direction of his work and the challenges he faced. From now on, the

Grammar School.
Cavendish
nr. Sudbury
Jan. 8. 1864

Francis Mr. Parker was my
Pupil Teacher at the "Barley
Church School", Herts, for 4 years,
and during that time was of
great use in my School &
a great comfort to myself.

He completed his Apprentice-
ship quite successfully, and
afterwards became a First Class
Queen's Scholar in St. Mark's
College, Chelsea.

He is a Sound & Consistent
Member of the Church of England,
intelligently holding & faithfully
teaching her doctrines, as she
teaches in her Book of Common

A testimonial of Francis Parker from Robert Hurst, his old employer at Barley, Hertfordshire.

story of Rolvenden's school gains a richer, deeper, and more human aspect.

He straightaway took up the mantle of his predecessor by becoming choirmaster at the church opposite. In his early years he records sending two or three choirboys out of school to assist with the singing at occasional church festivals such as those of St Paul, St Andrew or St John the Baptist. Parker was liked and respected by Rev. Rumsey, and if the headmaster was ever irked by the vicar's requests, such as for all boys to attend church every Friday morning during Lent (as was required in 1865), then he never showed it.

Francis Parker's constant bugbear – the one issue that would dog him for the rest of his career, with little if any relief – was the attendance question. He faced a constant daily battle to encourage his pupils to come to school regularly and punctually. Quite apart from irregular attendance slowing down the rate of progress in the school, it had a more prosaic effect. The annual government grant to a school was calculated partly on the average attendance of its pupils, and this grant made up a fair proportion of Mr Parker's salary. So the headmaster, as well as his school, was losing out. Much the same was true of Miss Tuer, who enjoyed the same arrangement and also suffered through the irregular attendance of the girls and infants.

For a rural parish, facing mild to severe agricultural depressions throughout the late Victorian era, there were several compelling reasons to keep children away from school. The older ones could be usefully put to work with their fathers, contributing to the household income. Others might be required to stay at home to look after the family's infants while their mother went to work. Tradition and convention in these villages was geared towards employment and away from education, with many of the poorest children finding reasons not to attend school for many months on end.

Consider the agricultural year in rural Kent: March and April saw hop-tying; the binding of plants to their lines in the hop-gardens, easily done by women and children. The traditional harvest ran through July and August, but in Kent the later harvest of hops also required labour in September and well into October, sometimes up to the end of the month depending on conditions. (Thus the long summer holiday for Kentish schools began and ended a good month later than in other parts of the country with more traditional crops.) After hopping came the foraging of chestnuts and acorns for animal feed; an occupation for the poorest families. The shooting season also saw opportunities for boys to serve as 'beaters,' driving the game towards the guns.

The original 1864 log book, held at the school.

The only window where children might attend school without diversion was between December and February – the high season for illness, not helped by discouraging weather which soaked poorly-clothed children to the skin on their long walks (sometimes nearly two miles) to school, causing chilblains and colds. Add to this the many distractions of country life – market fairs at Tenterden, Sandhurst, Hawkhurst and Benenden, cricket matches, the occasional travelling circus, the practice of girls parading garlands through the village on May Day, or boys carting effigies of Guy Fawkes on November 5th – and it is not surprising that attendance became an unresolvable issue, and the key frustration of Francis Parker's time at Rolvenden. His log books show that this was a preoccupation bordering on obsession.

Discipline through corporal punishment was commonplace, and there are many examples in the boys' log books: for stealing, for lying, for disobedience, for swearing, for fighting, for throwing stones, for going into the girls' schoolroom, for irreverence during Prayers. Though rarely specified, these punishments would have been meted out with a cane. But by the standards of the time it was not overbearing, and Mr Parker gives a sense that he regrets having to do so, and would not, were it neither justified nor worthwhile. Corporal punishment to girls was officially frowned upon, and Miss Tuer's usual sanction was to keep her children in during breaks.

The curriculum had widened slightly since Mr Oxley's time: the three R's (elementary subjects) were still paramount, and their examination accounted for most of the yearly government grant, but this income could be boosted by success in extra subjects. Mr Parker's choice was to teach his boys English grammar, geography and history. According to the requirements of the HMI examination, these last two were taught in a fashion reminiscent of Mr Gradgrind from Dickens' *Hard Times*: tedious lists of names and dates of monarchs and battles, given with very little context. Geography consisted only of naming and identifying various features (countries, principal settlements, mountain ranges, rivers, capes) on blank maps of Britain, Europe and the World.

Girls took on geography and needlework as their extra subjects, and the latter overwhelmed the timetable and was given great importance. Village women regularly brought their embroidery to the school for the girls to repair, and particularly good items were sold at vicarage fetes or entered for prizes at local fairs. It was a fiddly and time-consuming job to prepare and correct the girls' work for them, but if Miss Tuer received any help from other ladies in this regard – as happened in other villages – then it is not recorded.

About the only time when good attendance could be absolutely relied upon was the week leading up to the annual School Treat in August, before which the teachers would draw up a list of those eligible to attend. It was usually held at one or other of the larger village houses with land – such as Maytham Hall, Sparkeswood or Hole Park – and involved games, music, sports and a sumptuous tea laid on for up to 200 children.

The schoolroom was used for parish functions such as concerts, penny readings and dance classes. The mourners at the funeral of the village doctor made use of it in December 1864, and the church choir held their weekly practice there for no fee except the cost of heating and lighting. Rolvenden's Volunteer Rifle Corps also drilled regularly in the schoolroom, and Mr Parker's log book mentions an incident in December 1865 when a practical joker stole the keys and locked them inside. Presumably they managed to free themselves, and the keys were found by two schoolboys the following morning, hanging on a nearby door.

Three years into his tenure, Mr Parker's progress was such that he received official recognition from the government inspector, who stated that he was 'a very careful teacher' who had conducted the school 'with care and diligence.' The school roll was increasing, and with it, the amount of fees being paid, and the school managers unanimously voted him a donation of £5 in addition to his £50 salary for 1867. Emboldened by this vote of confidence he requested, and received, a pay rise for all subsequent years.

As numbers increased, defects in the school accommodation began to show. When attendance was good the schoolroom was uncomfortably crowded, and at the height of summer could be unbearably hot. Parker wrote in June 1867 that in the boys' room it was 'almost impossible to teach, the school being so badly built and ventilated.' Two large windows had been fitted without opening mechanisms, trapping the sun's heat without any relief. Things were little better in the girls' room, where Miss Tuer noted that the heat made needlework especially difficult with clammy fingers. Conversely, in winter the walls were mottled and damp, with a badly-fitting door letting the cold in – on at least one occasion the desks all had to be moved to the opposite side of the room to avoid the draught as far as possible. The poor state of the building was acknowledged for the first time, and a timely legacy of nearly £20 from the will of villager William Blackman allowed for some repairs to be made. But this did not solve the overcrowding issue, and the teachers and pupils struggled on in these conditions for another decade. A plan was proposed for the building of a separate schoolroom to accommodate 100 boys, with the existing one given over to infants, but this came to nothing.

In autumn 1870 came a brutal reminder of the danger of infectious diseases, particularly among children taught at close quarters. Young Amos Fuggle caught diphtheria and died on 17th October. His funeral two days later was attended by most of the boys in his class. More pupils soon caught it, and attendance dropped like a stone as parents kept their children away from school. But this precaution came too late for the Elphee family, whose sons James (aged 8), Henry (aged 5) and Robert (aged 6) all died one week after each other in November. Mr Parker recorded their names in his log book, drew a black border around the entries, and added 'R.I.P.' In all, Rolvenden's diphtheria epidemic of 1870 claimed 17 victims.

The following year the Elementary Education Act, known as the 'Forster Act' after its drafter, the Liberal MP William Forster, came into effect. The Act formalised the system of inspection and 'payment by results,' and also made provision for a school to be established in every parish where there was not currently an efficient one. These new schools would be 'board schools,' run by an elected district school board which would have the power to levy local taxes to fund their schools, which would be non-denominational. The church schools – such as that at Rolvenden – would not be interfered with, as long as they could prove themselves to be efficient. Government inspectors travelled the country, assessing both the standard of teaching and the size of the buildings required to accommodate all necessary children. It was on this latter point that most parishes fell short, and in the case of two Dame Schools in Rolvenden, run by Mrs Sherwood and Miss Chacksfield and consisting of nine children each, the inspector remarked that the rooms used were 'ridiculously small.' The verdict on the National School would arrive the following year.

Meanwhile Francis Parker had been courting Ann, the daughter of James Oxley, and the couple married in April 1871. Their first child, Edith, arrived the following year, with others at regular intervals: James, Francis, Arthur, Herbert, Sydney and John. All would at some stage be taught by their father in his school. It was a fitting continuation of a dynasty that had already served Rolvenden for nearly ninety years, and his marriage no doubt helped Mr Parker to inherit much of the affection and esteem still held towards Mr Oxley. That was where any similarity ended: Parker was the product of a new and stringent teacher training programme, closely regulated and without the considerable latitude his predecessor had enjoyed.

For example, the 1870 Act now required reading, writing and arithmetic to be taught according to a certain Standard, of which there were six:

STANDARD I

Reading — One of the narratives next in order after monosyllables in an elementary reading book used in the school.

Writing — Copy in manuscript character a line of print, and write from dictation a few common words.

Arithmetic — Simple addition and subtraction of numbers of not more than four figures, and the multiplication table to multiplication by six.

STANDARD II

Reading — A short paragraph from an elementary reading book.

Writing — A sentence from the same book, slowly read once, and then dictated in single words.

Arithmetic — The multiplication table, and any simple rule as far as short division (inclusive).

STANDARD III

Reading — A short paragraph from a more advanced reading book.

Writing — A sentence slowly dictated once by a few words at a time, from the same book.

Arithmetic — Long division and compound rules (money).

STANDARD IV

Reading — A few lines of poetry or prose, at the choice of the inspector.

Writing — A sentence slowly dictated once, by a few words at a time, from a reading book, such as is used in the first class of the school.

Arithmetic — Compound rules (common weights and measures).

STANDARD V

Reading — A short ordinary paragraph in a newspaper, or other modern narrative.

Writing — Another short ordinary paragraph in a newspaper, or other modern narrative, slowly dictated once by a few words at a time.

Arithmetic — Practice and bills of parcels.

STANDARD VI

Reading — To read with fluency and expression.

Writing — A short theme or letter, or an easy paraphrase.

Arithmetic — Proportion and fractions (vulgar and decimal).

Additional subjects in English grammar, geography, history and needlework continued, with the introduction of music, or more particularly singing, every morning. This consisted mostly of old English folk-songs taught and read according to tonic sol-fa, a rudimentary method whereby each note is sung according to its interval away from a starting note (the 'tonic'). Mr Parker was very proficient in this and his efforts were successful.

The verdict as to the school's efficiency arrived in July 1872 and caused some consternation. There was no issue whatever with the standard of teaching, and the fact that an extension was needed to accommodate all the

Francis Parker and his wife from 1871, Ann (née Oxley).

pupils comfortably came as no surprise. But it was ordered that this be done by providing two infants' schoolrooms, for 50 pupils each; one at the current school and one at Rolvenden Layne. The government's reasoning was that the Layne children were capable of walking a mile up to the Streyte once they were seven or eight years old, but not before then. The managers conferred and decided that the expense of providing a separate school was out of the question, and Rev. Rumsey was called upon to make the counter-arguments. With the aid of a shaded map, he submitted that one infants' schoolroom at the Streyte would be more central for all children of the parish, not just those at the Layne, but in other outlying parts (such as along the roads to Benenden and Hastings), and that most of the Layne children would be accompanied up to the Streyte by older children, often their siblings. These arguments won the day, and the Education Department relented, altering its requirement to a new infants' schoolroom for 100 pupils on the existing site.

By August 1873, the managers were ready to submit plans for the new building, together with a request for a conveyance to them of an extra piece of church land, behind the school house, which would form the new girls' and infants' playground. But this opened up another can of worms, as on inspection the original conveyance of 1837 was found to be defective. It took over a year of protracted legal wrangling to sort it out by re-establishing the school trust altogether, and by this time the original estimates for the work were out of date and had to be re-submitted. The managers, undaunted, set about the task of raising the £537 required for the project. This took a further year, but was achieved through a widespread canvassing of all the parishioners, who responded with enthusiasm. Chief among them was Frank Morrison of Hole Park, the son of a drapery magnate and Member of Parliament, who contributed a magnificent £100 which was matched as a grant by the Education Department.

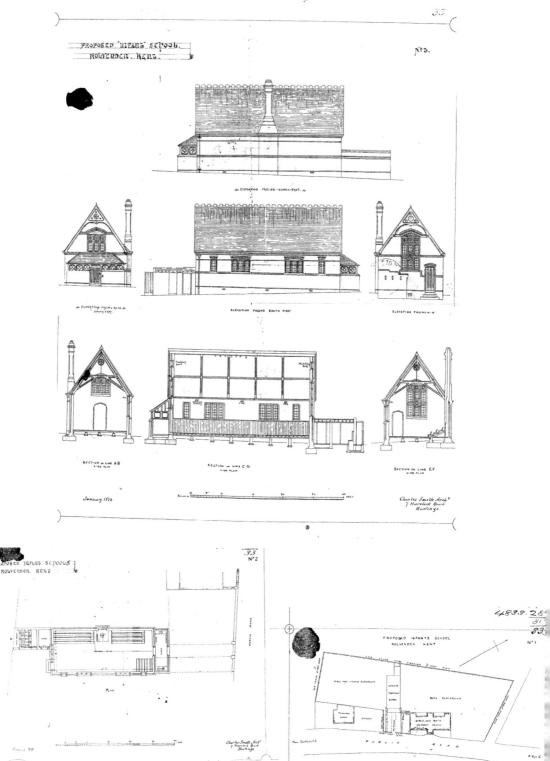

Charles Smith's 1873
plans for the new
infants' building.

The plans were drawn up by Charles Smith of Hastings in the Gothic Revival style much favoured at the time – a larger but comparable example being Wittersham School, completely rebuilt in 1874. It was originally envisaged that Rolvenden's new infant school would be sited to the southwest of the current building, roughly where the swimming pool is today. By the time building started in the summer of 1875 it had been re-sited to the northeast, for reasons unknown, but perhaps to avoid separating the girls' schoolroom from the girls' playground, and giving better and easier access to both. An advertisement was placed, seeking a certificated infants' teacher, and Esther Rosalie Williams – known as Rosa – was appointed to begin work on the agreed opening date of 31st January 1876. She was 21 years old, originally from Nottinghamshire, and a recent graduate of Bishop Otter Training College in Chichester.

It was not an easy start. Rev. Rumsey suffered an unspecified accident shortly before the opening day, was confined to bed and missed the celebrations – he was on crutches for some months. And while the building was ready on time, the teaching apparatus arrived four days late. But Miss Williams made the best of it, and the effect on the school was immediate. Relieved of the youngest children in her class, Miss Tuer's girls had more room and their teacher more time to devote to them. The rate of learning, and the tone and order of the girls, improved greatly.

The teachers had some hope that the attendance might also improve with the passing of the Agricultural Children Act in 1873, which banned the employment of those under eight years old. Children above this age could gain a Labour Pass by proving a minimum number of attendances at school during the year. This did not stop some people trying to contravene it:

> *March 19 [1875]. James Poile who is under 8 years of age went to work on Monday contrary to the permissions of the Agricultural Children Act. A notice to his employer brought him back on Tuesday morning. George Packham applied for a certificate under the same Act which was refused as he had not made his attendances.*

> *June 16 [1876]. Average is 63.3 for the week, exactly 13 more than last week. This increase is in a great measure due to the Agricultural Children Act under which Act the Policeman pays quarterly visits to all employers of labour so that all children who are at work contrary to the provisions of the Act are sent to school.*

Despite Mr Parker's enthusiasm, the Act was regarded as a failure and it was replaced by the Elementary Education Act 1876. Ironically, in Rolvenden at least, Parker found this new provision far less satisfactory:

> *April 27 [1877]. A great many boys are now at work and many are at work who ought to be at school. The Education Act of 1876 is at present being broken in many instances by boys under 9 years of age. Irregular attendance is now beginning to tell its tale. Out of 8 boys in the first class six failed in arithmetic this morning.*

May 4 [1877]. Farmers are now very busy and a great number of boys have left for the summer, some have left who ought to be at school and all are gone without a Labour Pass. School attendance committee has not yet been appointed though it is now May. The prospects of the school for the coming examination could hardly be worse. There are a few more boys who will most likely have to go to work so that we have not yet reached the worst.

June 22 [1877]. The attendance is now as bad as it can well be, worse than it was last summer. The Inspection is to be on Wednesday July 11. The prospects of the school are anything but rosy at present with the irregularity in attendance since Easter and the great number of boys now absent. Notices sent to several absentees on Thursday without any results.

Such was the desperation surrounding the inspector's verdict that attempts were made to persuade parents to send their children in to Rolvenden from afar, even if they were no longer on the school's books:

June 29 [1877]. George and Fred Wellstead unfortunately will leave the Parish before the day of Inspection and are going too far to be brought back.

May 17 [1878]. Sent to George and James Packham whose parents live at Benenden to try and induce them to send the boys to the examination. No answer yet received.

Not helping the situation was the constant threat of illness which could quickly turn serious. In February 1877 a case of smallpox was identified a mile from the school, and as a precaution the coins brought in by each child were put into a tub of Condy's Fluid, an early disinfectant. Very often the enemy was within, such as the following month when scarlet fever was found in a household a week after the first symptoms had appeared – during all of which time the son of the family had continued to attend school. In 1878 an outbreak of measles affected nearly all the children, causing the deaths of three infants. Miss Williams is known to have visited her sick pupils, but the teachers were constantly at risk of infection themselves, and Mr Parker's children Edith and James were themselves absent for several months during 1878 with whooping-cough. Only their father seemed immune from it all – in such circumstances his tenacity was remarkable, and according to the records he never appeared to take a day off.

If anything, the challenges of school life at Rolvenden renewed Parker's vigour, and the conclusions of the government and diocesan inspectors were seldom less than excellent. Any lapses called for positive action without blame – when the standard of needlework was judged to have dropped, the vicar's daughter Miss Rumsey came in regularly to help out, as she also did when knitting was introduced in 1877. Similarly, Miss Williams' younger sister Emily, also a student of Bishop Otter College, occasionally came to bolster the infants' teaching. Parker continued to keep a close watch on the conduct of his pupils:

April 13 [1877]. Admitted Albert White to the second standard from the Roman Catholic School at Tenterden, an addition to the school but certainly not an improvement. The language, manners and general behaviour of this boy are decidedly bad. A little wholesome discipline has somewhat tamed him and probably by this time next week he will cease to upset the school discipline.

June 15 [1877]. George Hyland, a little boy in the 4th class who was only admitted two or three weeks ago has been found out this week to be a thief. 7/4 found upon him on Tuesday which he had stolen from his mother. The future of this boy must be very closely watched.

As did Miss Williams, who for all her apparent kindliness, could only be pushed so far:

February 11 [1878]. Stephen Rope was entered on the books. To everything that he was told to do he said 'I baint' which is equivalent to 'I shall not,' so after spending a quarter of an hour with him and to no effect I used the pointer on his knuckles, which instantly procured obedience. He was no trouble for the rest of the day.

February 12 [1878]. The Vicar came in the morning and told me that Mrs Rope complained to him this morning that Stephen had been punished. The doctor, who happened to be at the vicarage, examined the boy and said there was no trace whatever of the boy having been caned.

The above episode points to a growing trend. Whereas previously most parents and guardians had been supportive – in June 1876 a mother actually requested that Mr Parker caned her two sons for their truancy – a few short years later, some had begun to actively resist, making the teachers' work harder:

November 7 [1879]. Punished Alice Vincett for disobedience. Visit from her grandfather in consequence, in spite of which the punishment has evidently done her good.

January 9 [1880]. Punished William Adams for bad behaviour during lessons on Wednesday morning. His guardians think the punishment excessive and have kept him from school the rest of the week.

April 23 [1880]. Punished Ernest Brunger (Standard III) for disobedience. He had been absent 5 weeks so was greatly in want of wholesome correction, a fair amount of which he received. He was kept away till Thursday when he returned.

June 5 [1880]. Fanny Whatman (Standard II) foolishly withdrawn from school. She failed in two subjects at the examination and has been withdrawn because she was to go in Standard II another year.

June 3 [1881]. Sent Emily and Jack Maynard home for their school money this morning after receiving a note from their mother informing me she should pay when and how she chose.

November 11 [1881]. Punished Thomas James for disobedience. Angry interview with his mother afterwards, both boys absent today.

Much of this attitude came down to the fact that attendance at school and payment for it, both compulsory but hitherto easily flouted, were now being enforced by the hated Attendance Officer. In the Tenterden district this was Robert Dunk, whose role involved calling on the homes of children who had not attended school the previous week, according to a list given to him by Mr Parker. Mr Dunk enjoyed some early success but the Attendance Committee who appointed him were always reluctant to prosecute infringers. When parents were summoned before the Cranbrook magistrates, fines were often nominal and far less than the income a working child brought to a household. Bearing the brunt of both the parents' contempt and the teachers' frustration was the unfortunate Mr Dunk, about whom even the mild-mannered Mr Parker was scathing:

June 18 [1880]. The attendance is much below what it really ought to be if absentees were properly looked up instead of being allowed to come and go as they please.

August 26 [1880]. Unless the Attendance Officer does his work better after the holidays, the average must be considerably less than last year.

October 8 [1880]. Admitted Beatrice Bryant [who has] never been to school before though she is old enough to be in Standard II at least. This is the way the Attendance Committee and the Attendance Officer do their work.

November 5 [1880]. Attendance Officer still makes no sign whatever though there is plenty for him to do. Bye laws still a dead letter.

August 19 [1881]. The late Attendance Officer paid one or two visits to the school between Oct 1 [and] Mar 25 so these will be the only visits we have had from that exceedingly useful official for a whole year.

Julia Bull, infants' mistress from 1878.

This last comment refers to the fact that Mr Dunk left his position in March 1881, and it took a whole ten months for a replacement to be appointed – during which time, inevitably, the school attendance plumbed new depths.

Meanwhile the school itself was being re-ordered. Rosa Williams left in August 1878; she went on to teach in Ely, Edmonton and Barnet, where she gave up teaching to become a scripture reader, and died in 1916, aged 62. Her replacement at Rolvenden was 22-year-old Julia Bull from Hoxton, in the East End of London, but latterly working in Frome, Somerset. In Rolvenden she took up lodgings with Mary Bourner, who was also Miss Tuer's landlady, so the two teachers both lived and worked together. Miss Bull was a particularly diligent teacher who earned much praise from the inspector, and was regularly granted a bonus by the managers. It would therefore have been hard to take if her infants class had lost their newly-built room, which was being discussed by the managers at the time of her arrival. Because Mr Parker's class of older boys was the largest, the inspector recommended that they be moved into the spacious new infants' room and *vice versa*. This, however, was abandoned in favour of a later plan to conduct the older boys and girls as a 'mixed' school – that is, that Mr Parker would teach the oldest boys and girls together, Miss Tuer the middle class, and Miss Bull the infants as before.

Over forty years of segregated education at the National School, where boys and girls entered through separate doors, learned in separate classrooms, and played in separate playgrounds, was about to end.

The earliest known photograph of the school, from 1876, showing Francis Parker and his boys' division.

Friday. The Schools have this week been worked as one Mixed School as H. M. Inspector recommended. The Average No. of Boys is 62.7 Girls 43.6 Total 106.3. Weather very hot especially in the afternoon. Worked hard to make the new Arrangement run smoothly. The order at present is very bad. It is difficult to get the girls into good ways of doing their work at present another week or two will make a great difference to the work of the School. Taught the children to sing "Be gentle when at play"

Friday The Average this week for the Mixed School is Boys 62.8 Girls 44.7 Total 107.5. Worked hard this week at the Standard work. Discipline still very bad as the Mixed School is not yet in good working order, though the order is better than last week there is still a good deal too much noise during lessons and especially when lessons are being changed. Began to teach the School Sang "The sea-boy" on Thursday. Worked has at the grammar & geography in Stands II - VI Stand I contains many backward children

Chapter 4

A MIXED SCHOOL

1879-1900

THE MIXED SCHOOL came into being in July 1879, with the intention of carrying it on as an experiment for one year. While Miss Tuer took it in her stride, Mr Parker seems to have found coping with girls a particular challenge:

> *August 1 [1879]. Worked hard to make the new arrangement run smoothly. The order at present very bad. It is difficult to get the girls into good ways of doing their work at present; another week or two will make a great difference to the work of the school.*

> *October 31 [1879]. The girls do not yet fall into the discipline of the boys' school, aware many of them inclined to be troublesome... corporal punishment is in some cases necessary though most undesirable.*

> *November 21 [1879]. Punished several boys for throwing snowballs into the infants' school, though the girls were by far the worst.*

Nonetheless, these problems were ironed out and the new scheme remained. It did not alter the fact that the original schoolroom – now consisting of Mr Parker's senior pupils and Miss Tuer's middle class – was still 'ill-ventilated and virtually overcrowded,' in the words of the government inspector. He recommended that the youngest of Miss Tuer's pupils (at Standard I) be taught with the infants, where there was more room, but this was resisted by the managers.

Such conditions helped the spread of infectious disease, which came to another head in the autumn and winter of 1881-2. The death of seven-year-old Elvina Harden in the last week of the summer term, which Mr Parker recorded with real emotion, gave a foretaste of what was to come:

> *August 26 [1881]. Vina Harden, Standard II, died of diphtheria on Wednesday after one week's illness, to be buried tomorrow. Luckily schools break up today... Vina was present at school on Tuesday Aug 16, on Wednesday August 24th she was dead. R.I.P. She was a great favourite with all, teachers and scholars, and is terribly missed.*

Another death followed in the New Year (Emily Britcher, also aged seven) and by mid-January 1882 Parker's own children were all suffering. Inevitably, but for the only time in his career, the headmaster himself fell ill and the school was closed for two weeks. It reopened for two days before being closed again by order of the Medical Officer of Health, who demanded that the whole building be disinfected. Despite this disruption, that year's inspection verdict – which Parker had particularly feared – was as good as ever.

After four years of sterling work Miss Bull married a schoolmaster, becoming Mrs John Mockford, and left Rolvenden in July 1882 to start a family – her last government inspection praised her painstaking manner and careful teaching. Her husband was appointed headmaster of the school at Waddesdon, Buckinghamshire, and two children were born and raised there. The family transferred to Dinas Powys in South Wales at the end of 1887, while Julia was expecting a third child, but here tragedy struck. She developed complications and, while the infant son survived a difficult birth in January 1888, his mother died of a *postpartum* haemorrhage at the age of 31.

Jessie Atwick Ollis, aged 26 and from Gloucestershire, took up her position as infants' mistress in October 1882. She arrived at a time of some upheaval: a new Education Code was introduced, which determined the manner in which lessons were to be taught and demanded a greater standard than before to secure the same grant. Parker feared the worst, and sure enough, the inspection of 1883 heralded a reduction in the money received, and added more pressure for the accommodation to be revised:

> *The Master of this school continues to work with untiring energy, but his powers are, I fear, overtasked. If the first Standard were transferred to the Infants' School, where there is plenty of room for them, the Mixed School would gain greatly both from a sanitary and an educational point of view. The present arrangement is most unsatisfactory and most unnecessary... Unless this plan is adopted it is doubtful whether HM*

Inspector will be able to recommend any merit grant in future to the mixed school.

Mr Parker could not but show his frustration and anger:

> *The report of HM Inspector has been received this week and is the worst we have ever had... The hardest year's work done in the school has only produced these very meagre results, grant £7 less than last year and the Standard work is described as 'poor.' A lot of our time has been devoted to the children and this is the result of it all. The new Code will prove a dreadful disappointment to most country teachers and is very much too hard for country schools... Harder work for less grant cannot be considered a satisfactory state of things for either teachers or managers.*

As if to crown a dreadful year, an epidemic of scarlet fever broke out in August, grew steadily and caused the school to be closed for the whole of December. It did not die out completely until the following spring. By then, the school and village had sustained a great loss with the death of Rev. Rumsey, who died in March 1884. Mr Parker conducted the choir at his funeral, which attracted huge crowds of mourners, and for which the school was closed. Rumsey had supported the school for nearly 30 years, both as a careful and diligent manager, and as a gentle influence in his teaching of scripture to the children. It was largely thanks to his efforts that the infants' school was built despite many unexpected difficulties, and he is known to have paid the fees of at least one poor child to attend the school – there were certainly others.

Still, for reasons of money or otherwise, some parents held out against the system and resisted sending their children to school:

> *May 18 [1883]. The Attendance Officer perhaps does his best to see parents and employers but they tell him to his face they shall not obey and so the matter rests...*

> *August 3 [1883]. It is now about 3 months since a list was sent in [to the Attendance Committee]. The average of course is suffering but it is better to have no compulsion at all than compulsion that is only a sham. To tell parents they* must *send their children to school and then when they flatly refuse* not *to make them is a sham.*

> *December 31 [1883]. Worked hard this week and gave all the children in Standards III, IV, V and VI sums for home lessons but some parents object even to this and so make the work much harder. A great deal of wholesome pressure ought to be put upon parents, so far they have had none at all. The pressure has all been upon the teacher.*

Others continued to resent Parker's efforts at discipline:

> *January 9 [1885]. Found 4 dirty, abominable words written on the wall of School Closet, charged Arthur Funnell with writing them, who denied it but afterwards went and told two boys he did it. Punished him on Tuesday, message from his mother on Wednesday, threatening me with*

Ann Parker (centre) in 1887 with her children; (l-r) James, Edith, John, Sydney (sitting), Arthur, Francis, Herbert.

something dreadful, sent word back why he was punished, have heard no more about it.

March 13 [1885]. Punished Charles Funnell on Thursday for throwing stones at the school door, stormy interview with his father afterwards, both Funnells away all day today.

Tenterden's Attendance Committee, in Parker's eyes, continued to be either negligent or corrupt:

March 6 [1885]. Proceedings have been taken against two parents, one of whom was fined 2/6, the other got off altogether. The children for whose absence a parent was fined 2/6 had made <u>19 attendances</u> out of a possible <u>196</u>, not much encouragement for the Attendance Committee or their Officer to take proceedings against the parents.

March 27 [1885]. Chas Brunger illegally employed by Mr Avery, Guardian and probably a member of the School Attendance Committee... List of absentees sent to the Attendance Officer as usual but the whole thing is a farce from beginning to end, magistrates and Attendance Committees do as little as possible.

By 1885, on the rare occasions when attendance could be said to be good, Parker had to cope with 100 children in his classroom. A monitress – whose name is sadly unrecorded – was engaged for the first time to take charge of the 30 or so children in Standard I. Despite all their challenges the staff achieved acceptably good inspection reports; though Parker had exacting standards, and he never felt they quite reached the heights their efforts deserved. Aiming for better overall results, the girls stopped taking geography in favour of even more needlework, which was a particular strength. Other incentives were used, too: at Christmas 1885 a concert was given by the children to raise money for a magic lantern to be used for their entertainment.

Jessie Ollis moved on and was replaced in the infants' class by Florence Willett from Dorset, who began in January 1886. Her arrival at Rolvenden coincided with a new challenge to attendance: that of Primrose Day, held to celebrate the conservative values of Benjamin Disraeli and marked on 19th April each year since his death. Primroses for buttonholes were in great demand and a new industry sprung up in the Home Counties, whereby the flowers were collected in the preceding weeks and shipped to London. This was a lucrative trade for children and their families, but coming as it did just a few weeks before the inspector's visit in May, it became another reason for Mr Parker to despair. Within a couple of years the school would be almost empty throughout the first half of April.

A particularly severe agricultural depression occurred towards the end of the decade, and the records show that the poorest families were feeling the pinch:

> *October 19 [1888]. Sent John Poile home for his pence – no attendances since.*
>
> *December 7 [1888]. Paines absent all the week, sent home for their money and did not come back again. John Bryant also absent for the same cause.*
>
> *May 31 [1889]. Edwin Hyland sent home for his money on Monday, has not been to school since. Several others must be sent home next week unless the money is paid.*
>
> *January 31 [1890]. John and Rose Button absent all the week, also Elizabeth Hyland. All these children were sent home for their school money and did not return.*

In 1890 Attendance Enquiry Forms were introduced, designed to be made up by the Attendance Officer each Friday and sent to the parents of any children who had been absent that week. But Parker noted that the 'Attendance Officer cannot do much as there are no prosecutions. Much better to do without his help if possible,' and instead filled them out and sent them himself every evening. The prospect of receiving ten each week (five morning and five afternoon sessions) seems to have focused the minds of the most irregular attendees, and combined with incentives such as magic lantern shows, treats at Christmas, and attendance medals specially ordered from Birmingham, the situation – at last – improved. The inspector was gratified to see this, even if it was a notorious scramble to get as many pupils as possible to attend his examination. In May 1891 the weather was so bad on exam day that a covered van was sent round the village to collect the most distant children.

The monitress for Standard I was replaced in April 1892 by an appointed mistress, Louisa Eade, from Surrey but previously teaching at St Margaret-at-Cliffe. This was not without difficulty – it took six weeks of advertising before anyone applied for the role, and Miss Eade stayed for only ten weeks. Parker later sighed that her help would have been most useful, given the improvement in attendance. He also had a new challenge in that the boys were now required to be taught drawing – that is, technical drawing, rather than art – which ate into the time used for the more traditional subjects. When the inspector was critical Parker grumbled 'No allowance whatever [is] made for 5 or 6 hours weekly that have been spent on drawing and this time of course has been taken from the time spent on ordinary work. School days do not get longer and the time was fully used up before.'

Added to this, the rest of the staff were encountering problems. The effects of age and ill-health were beginning to tell on Miss Tuer, now 61 years old. She was compelled to take time off work during 1892 and the burden of teaching her class fell to Mr Parker, already overworked in his. A new assistant for Standard I was found who rejoiced in the name of Miss Margaret Thatcher but, like her predecessor, does not appear to have stayed more than a few months. Miss Willett, too, was struggling in the infants' class. The inspector recorded sternly that her pupils were:

> '… talkative, fidgety and inattentive, and loll about in all kinds of lazy attitudes. It is to be hoped that these serious faults will be corrected during the coming year, as otherwise the school will run a serious risk of being declared inefficient at the next Inspection.

Miss Willett was a competent and valued teacher but lacked the necessary skill to keep order and discipline among the smallest children. The obvious solution was to move her into Miss Tuer's role with the middle class on the latter's resignation, which occurred in March 1894 after 38 years and three months' diligent service to the school. She was presented with a clock, paid for by a collection among the staff and pupils. After living in Rolvenden throughout her life and career, in retirement Emily Tuer moved away to live with her sister Arabella, whose husband was a successful businessman on the King's Road in Chelsea, and later Fulham. She died there in 1905, aged 74.

After Miss Tuer's retirement the staff under Mr Parker went through a period of continual upheaval. The role of infants' mistress was first taken by Miss Annie Binnington, possibly from Yorkshire, who succeeded in improving the discipline of her class but stayed only a little over a year. She was replaced in October 1895 by Miss Celia Harris, originally from Harrietsham but lately working as a domestic servant in Folkestone. She encountered the same issues as Miss Willett and was brought up on the order of her pupils by the inspector. Ill-health forced her resignation a year later; she married and settled in East Ham with two children, but died in 1912, aged only 39. Throughout this time the Standard I assistant teacher was Miss Edith Hogben from Smeeth, but in May 1896 Parker records that she has suddenly 'resigned her assistantship and left this day of her own accord' – there is perhaps an untold story there. Miss Hogben went to teach at Sandgate but later left the profession to run a newsagent's shop in Folkestone. She died in 1934, aged 59.

Replacing Miss Harris in the infants' class was Miss Florence Ruby, from Northwood in Middlesex, who also struggled with maintaining order and resigned after nine months in August 1897. It seems though that she was prevailed upon to stay, and did so, withdrawing her resignation and returning in October. However she suffered a serious illness the following summer and left for good in August 1898. Despite her ill-health she continued as a schoolteacher in London and died in Surrey in 1956, aged 82. Florence Willett left Rolvenden and the teaching profession in June 1897 to get married. (The Willett family tree is particularly entangled – Florence married her first cousin, as had her parents before her. Another cousin was William Willett, who successfully campaigned for the adoption of British Summer Time.) She died in Surrey in 1952, aged 90. Her position at Rolvenden was taken by Miss Laura Nokes, born in Finsbury but lately living at Towyn in North Wales, where her father was the schoolmaster. She possessed a 'very quiet reverent manner,' but this unfortunate lady is known to have suffered from fragile health, both mentally and physically, and was the subject of some interest in October 1888, aged 15, when she disappeared from home and was found unconscious and soaking wet on the beach at Colwyn. She recovered from this experience, said to have been caused by 'a derangement of the mind... brought about by a too close application to study.'

Two Victorian glass inkwells used at the school, now held by Tenterden and District Museum.

Throughout these staff worries Parker recorded how the wider situation in agriculture continued to bear down on his school, and demonstrated his social conscience:

> *March 15 [1895]. Boys are now beginning to leave for the summer's work and as there has been so much distress during the winter every boy who can earn the smallest wages is wanted by his parents.*

> *October 11 [1895]. Many boys leaving. This is partly owing to the agricultural depression. Four farms each containing more than 100 acres are not employing a single labourer – one of the four only about a year ago found employment for 5 men besides boys and lads. This must surely affect school attendance during the winter months.*

> *November 1 [1895]. Agricultural depression is playing sad havoc with the attendance this year. Nothing like the present state of things has ever been known in this part of Kent. Numbers of men are out of work.*

Very rarely did Mr Parker display any righteous anger, but the avoidable death of a seven-year-old pupil caused him to lose his reserve:

> *January 24 [1896]. Charles Crump, Standard I, died on Wednesday night of croup and bronchitis after just one week's illness. The death of this poor boy was no doubt accelerated by insufficient food. There are 6 children – the father was out of work last year 13 consecutive weeks, he*

has had very little work this summer and has been a good deal out of work since hop-picking – at present earning alone 12/ per week out of which 8 persons live! Rent and living cost at least 3/6 per week. This in Christian England – and while there are people not far off living in luxury.

Undoubtedly Parker took a great interest in his pupils, and was mindful of their wellbeing. He was generally able to command the respect of the unlikeliest candidates, and records how in June 1899 he admitted a boy named Oliver Sweet, lately of Sissinghurst, who had played truant there for two months. During his first week at Rolvenden he did not attend a single session, went missing on the Wednesday evening and was found the following morning at Cranbrook Police Station. Seven days later, Parker was able to record that he had successfully brought the boy round, and that he had achieved perfect attendance for the whole of the previous week – probably for the first time in years. By now Miss May Howard had joined the staff as infants' mistress, replacing Florence Ruby. Miss Nokes left in July 1899; she returned to Wales, where she died in 1911, aged 38. Her replacement in the middle class was Miss Lena Winwood, born in Exeter but previously teaching at Woodchurch School.

Through the last few months of 1899 the writing in Parker's log book becomes almost indecipherable. His attitudes are still present – he reports on the employer of a persistent absentee being fined 'the magnificent sum of one shilling… what a farce!!' – but he has become absent-minded and repetitive; it is clear that he is burnt out. His last entry is on 21st December, and four days later he led the carol singers around the village on Christmas morning as usual. On 2nd January he suddenly sickened and his son James was brought in to deputise when the school reopened a few days later. Francis Parker saw only a week of the new year. He died on 8th January 1900, aged 56. The school was closed for his send-off three days later, when 'a great number of the children attended the funeral of their beloved master.' One week after this, James was appointed headteacher of the school his father had served so faithfully for 36 years.

ROLVENDEN.
DEATH OF MR PARKER.

The death of Mr F. W. Parker, on the 8th inst, at the age of 56, has deprived Rolvenden of a conscientious and highly esteemed public servant. Mr Parker, who received his training at S. Mark's College, Chelsea, was appointed National Schools master in 1864, succeeding the late Mr James Oxley, and marrying, a few years later, his predecessor's eldest daughter. As time went on, various local offices including Assistant Overseer, Secretary of the Rolvenden and Newenden Conservative Association, Parish Clerk, Collector of Income Tax and Clerk to the Parish Council, became added to Mr Parker's primary work, but his energy, business capacity and geniality enabled him to perform all his duties with regularity and efficiency, and with never-failing courtesy and consideration, and many have lost a friend sincere and true.

For more than 20 years Mr Parker was the right hand of the late revered Vicar, Mr Rumsey, in the Church Choir, and spared no pains or cost of scanty leisure to maintain it after Mr Rumsey's death in the efficiency which had become a Rolvenden tradition. Mr Parker was only taken ill on the night of Tuesday, the 2nd inst, and as lately as Christmas morning conducted his carol singers round the village as he had done for many years, and may therefore be said to have died in harness. An especially sad feature of the event was the coincident serious illness of Mrs Parker who was unable to be at her dying partner's bedside.

The funeral took place on Thursday, 11th inst, when a large number of the inhabitants were present, including the Misses Rumsey, Miss Windwood (Girls' School Mistress), Miss Howard (Infants' School Mistress), Mrs Harden, Mrs and the Misses Robson, Mrs Huggins, Mrs Smith and Miss Piper, Mr T. Morfee and Capt Badger (Churchwardens), Messrs Hilder, Harden, Cook, Dudley, Button and Thompson (members of the Parish Council), the members of the old choir, and Messrs W. Burden, sen, W. Burden, jun, J. Wicken, E. Wicken, T. Geering, F. Geering, H. Geering, W. Drawbridge, J. Bridgland, T. Cheesman, J. Beeken, J. Stedman, J. Cook, T. Huggins, W. Phillips, W. Miles, T. Robson, and P. R. Ward ; Dr Skinner, Mr H. S. Norton, Mr W. B. Hook, and Mr Macdonald (Tenterden), Rev W. M. C. Clarke (Vicar of S. Michael's, Tenterden), Miss Wenman and Mr Gibbs (Benenden). The service, which was of the plainest description, was impressively read by the Vicar, Rev H. P. Smith. The coffin was of polished oak, and bore the inscription :

FRANCIS WILLIAM PARKER,
Born 27th Dec, 1843,
Died 8th Jan, 1900.

Many beautiful wreaths were sent. The funeral arrangements were successfully conducted by Mr D. Russell.—We are pleased to state that Mrs Parker is improving, although it is slowly.

Chapter 5

BRAVE NEW WORLD

1900-18

JAMES PARKER HAD been born at School House on Christmas Day 1873, baptised at St Mary's church opposite, and educated in his father's school. Unlike his father, he gained a wealth of outside experience before taking up his position at Rolvenden. He was a pupil teacher at Bethersden School from 1888-9 before transferring to the British School at Ashford – roles that gave him experience of non-church schools in both a village and town setting. He then spent three years as an uncertificated assistant teacher at Epsom Church School in Surrey before studying for a teaching certificate at his father's old college, St Mark's in Chelsea. When recalled to Rolvenden in 1900, he was in his fourth year of teaching at Holy Trinity Boys' School in Eastbourne.

He had an insider's knowledge, both as a pupil and his father's son, of the challenges that faced Rolvenden School, and set about solving them in his own way. While not as vociferous about it, he concurred with his father's low opinion of the Attendance Officer. Instead an 'attendance banner' was introduced, held by a different class each week 'to encourage the children to attend regularly and to encourage a healthy rivalry between the different classes.' While enjoying some moderate success, it did not prevent the issue of children being illegally employed, such as beating during the shooting season, or delivering telegrams for the Post Office.

Rev. Harry Percival Smith, vicar of Rolvenden 1896-1904.

Incentives were continued with a summer treat, on more than one occasion hosted at Great Maytham Hall by Mrs Townsend, the married name of writer Frances Hodgson Burnett. The then vicar, Rev. Harry Percival Smith (who was distinctly unimpressed with Mrs Townsend's private life) was a proponent of the Arts and Crafts movement, and hand-carved new pews for the church which remain *in situ* today. When they were dedicated after many years' hard work, the children were given the day off school to attend and celebrate. In addition to the card and orange handed out at Christmas, the children now received a packet of sweets from Mr Sackville Cresswell of Hole Park, who also gave a magic lantern show specifically to encourage attendance.

Miss Howard left the infants' department shortly after James Parker's arrival and was replaced by Mrs Lucy Dinn, aged 41 and originally from Newington, south London. Her arrival had been brought about by tragedy – her husband Joseph, the headmaster of Theydon Garnon School in Essex, had died only six weeks previously, also aged 41; this sad event not only bereaving his family but depriving his wife of her position as schoolmistress. She dutifully applied for the position at Rolvenden and settled with her children at the cottage nearest the west door of the church – now 20 Hastings Road. At the same time a local boy, Fred Blandford, was recorded as the first named paid monitor, and he was later joined in the infants' class by Edith Mills, followed by Annie Russell and then Frances Goble.

Mrs Lucy Dinn (extreme right) with her children at 20 Hastings Road.

The early part of the century saw a boom of interest in cricket, and a new school team was refounded in 1901, going on to play several matches a year. In addition, and as a response to the Boer War, all pupils were required to practise militaristic 'drill' exercises in the playground once a week, and they were regularly inspected by serving officers based locally. A little later, Mr Parker suggested that a violin teacher be allowed to tutor pupils in the school, and it was agreed by the managers to let him do so free of charge.

The younger Mr Parker continued his father's approach to discipline and particularly corporal punishment – that is, sparingly, but never doubting its necessity. Cases included four infant boys caught stealing eggs, general bad behaviour, insolence during Prayers, and the perennial truancy. He had particular trouble with the Levitt family of the Layne who were habitual truants but, when they did attend, came in such a ragged and verminous condition that they were described as 'not fit to be with other children' – one time, by the village doctor himself. It was only on the threat of a letter to the county authorities that the situation improved at all.

James Parker married fellow teacher Annie Toop in Hampshire in the summer of 1902, and his new wife moved into the schoolhouse. Four sons – James, Arthur (known as Donald), Sydney (known as Thomas) and Philip – would arrive at regular intervals over the subsequent nine years, and all would eventually pass through their father's school, as their father had done before them.

By this time the government was trying to reconcile the fact that, while voluntary church schools educated one-third of British children, they were struggling through being funded entirely by donations. There remained a huge divide with the board schools, who were generally in a far better financial state because they could impose local taxes to raise funds. This difference had a visible effect on the quality of education, and board schools began to outperform their church equivalents.

James Parker with wife Annie (née Toop) and sons Donald and James, November 1906.

Prime Minister Arthur Balfour championed the 1902 Education Act to reduce this inequality by bringing all schools under a degree of state control, without compromising the nature of each one. The school boards were abolished and replaced with Local Education Authorities – in Kent's case, run by the county council from 1st July 1903, when they took over Rolvenden National School, which subsequently became known as Rolvenden Church of England School. These administered the local taxes and allowed a proportion to go to church schools. They were also responsible for paying all schoolteachers and providing appropriate materials such as books and furniture. In return, the churches had a responsibility for maintaining their school buildings and allowing the LEA's use of them as a school free of charge.

There were teething troubles with the new regime. An HMI inspection in 1904 criticised the condition and number of desks in the infants' class – but when the managers applied to the Kent Education Committee for new desks, they were refused. At least this complaint was justified. Later that year a do-gooder brought the attention of the Committee to the state of the school lavatories. They dispatched the District Surveyor to inspect them, who found them 'quite sweet and clean... They are thoroughly cleaned out each week and earth and disinfectant are liberally thrown down.'

Miss Winwood left in June 1905 to get married and was presented with a silver-plated cake basket; she became Mrs Burden and settled in Headcorn

James and Annie Parker, son John, and Miss Lena Winwood (centre, in doorway) at School House, January 1906.

with her new family, though she occasionally returned to teach at Rolvenden during times of staff illness. She remained in Headcorn for the rest of her life, and died in 1966, aged 92. Replacing Miss Winwood was not straightforward, and came at a time when HMI were still noting that the school was overcrowded and the staff, while competent, were overworked. Miss Norah Gibbs came temporarily, with Mrs Dinn's 15-year-old daughter Phoebe helping out as an apprentice teacher. Eventually Miss Bertha Preston was appointed, but could not begin until the autumn, so James Parker's wife Annie was drafted in to help. To aid with the overcrowding in the infants' class the gallery of tiered seating was removed and a local girl, Rose Ovenden, was taken on as a supplementary teacher for a few months.

On 12th October 1905 a boy named Sydney Walton attended school as usual in the morning, then during the lunch hour went with some friends to the grounds of Great Maytham Hall to look for chestnuts – whether for animal feed or for a game of 'conkers' was never established. He climbed a tree but slipped and fell 17 feet to the ground; with the aid of his friends, he was able to walk home, but died of a haemorrhage that afternoon. The incident 'cast a great gloom over the whole school,' in Mr Parker's words, and many were absent to attend the boy's funeral four days later.

Mrs Dinn decided that she was better suited to teaching slightly older children, and so was moved to Standard I with a certificated teacher, Miss Florence Watson, taking charge of the infants from May 1906. Both teachers shared the infants' classroom, and the Kent Educational Committee was applied to for the cost of a partition to separate the classes, but they answered that it was for the school managers to provide. Consequently, nothing was done, and conditions became less and less satisfactory to both teachers. It was not helped – ironically – by attendance being so good; the Tenterden Attendance Committee awarding medals and certificates to those pupils who achieved over 98% attendance during the year.

Also in 1906 came the first celebration of Empire Day on 24th May – the birthday of the late Queen Victoria. Each child was given a slice of cake and small box of chocolates.

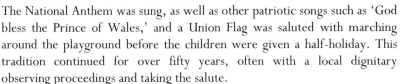

Attendance medals 1907-18, issued at Rolvenden and now held by Tenterden and District Museum.

The National Anthem was sung, as well as other patriotic songs such as 'God bless the Prince of Wales,' and a Union Flag was saluted with marching around the playground before the children were given a half-holiday. This tradition continued for over fifty years, often with a local dignitary observing proceedings and taking the salute.

Miss Preston left Rolvenden that November. Her replacement in the middle class was to become a legendary character, still fondly remembered today. Miss Daisy Close was then 27 years old; born in Suffolk to two teachers, she was the eldest of five children, all of whom followed their parents into the same profession. By 1906 she was living in Northiam, where her father was headmaster of the village school, and on obtaining her new job she took lodgings at Rolvenden. Miss Close became a feature of the village very quickly; it was recognised that she had a gift for teaching and she was universally respected by her pupils, many of whom kept up a correspondence with her long after they had left her care. As is often the

Miss Daisy Close and her Standard IV class, 1908.

case, such respect was earned by an insistence on learning conscientiously and thoroughly, and the threat, or use, of punishment when it was merited. Miss Close's method of choice was a hazel cane she had made herself, about two-and-a-half feet in length and half an inch thick, which was employed on the hand of the errant pupil. Even when not used, it was an effective deterrent to bad behaviour – stories filtered down from older to younger children, and those who never saw the hazel cane knew where it was kept. For those requiring less stringent correction, a round ruler was used to tap knuckles, particularly if a pen was not being held at the correct angle. She encouraged the neatest possible attitude in handwriting and stitching, with a keen eye for unevenness.

The firm hand of Miss Close came just as another crisis with the staff was looming. Miss Watson, Mrs Dinn and Phoebe Dinn – of whom only Miss Watson was a certificated teacher – had over 70 infants to teach between them. Under the intense pressure, Miss Watson's health failed and she resigned in March 1907. She was replaced by 25-year-old Miss Grace Herring, originally from Hornsea in Essex. Steps were put in place to appoint an extra uncertificated teacher and Miss Edith Morley was appointed to begin in January 1908.

But no sooner had Miss Morley arrived in the New Year than Mrs Dinn was suddenly called away: her son Henry had been taken ill and died at the age of 25. On her return, she found that the numbers in the infants' division were so high that Mr Parker required her to work there, rather than in Standard I as before – which was given over to Miss Morley. No doubt still raw from her loss, she refused his instructions and resigned, defiantly seeing out her notice period in Standard I while Miss Morley helped with the infants instead. It was a sour note on which to end eight years' service, and to cap it

Misses Herring and Morley and the infants' division, 1908.

off, her daughter Phoebe's apprenticeship ended at the same time, so two teachers were lost. But by a quirk of fate, Mrs Dinn's replacement was unable to take up her position due to ill health, and Phoebe Dinn was offered the post. There were no hard feelings, it seems. Her mother went to live in Epping and emigrated to New York the following year, only to return to England within a few years. After a spell in Cresswell near Sheffield she retired to West Yorkshire, and died near Keighley in 1945, aged 86.

Miss Phoebe Dinn.

Phoebe Dinn was, by all accounts, a great success at Rolvenden in the vital early years of schooling. Bessie Heasman (Jenner) recounted in 1987:

> I well remember my first teacher, Miss Phoebe Dinn, whom I adored. She was a most kind and caring teacher. She taught us the basics of school life, and taught us such lovely little songs, and was so helpful with our first lessons. I am sure so many, like me, were very happy and loved our school days with her.

To stem the number of children wishing to join, the managers decided to admit no new pupils under five years old, and to appoint a monitress – Bertha Goble – to help Miss Herring with those under-fives already in the school. But no amount of reordering could disguise the fact that the present accommodation was too small and needed extending, and this began to be explored by the end of 1909.

As ever, money was the issue – the first estimate for the new classroom came in at £450, with every prospect that it would increase. A good deal of discontent was stirred up when it was suggested that the overcrowding was partly due to the large number of children from Dr Barnardo's and the Waifs and Strays Societies living in the parish. The hospitality and generosity of Rolvenden in this regard was causing an unforeseen consequence, it seemed – surely these societies might at least contribute to the cost of a new classroom? The managers agreed to ask them but were politely rebuffed in both cases. To add to the pressure, the government decreed that each child was to be allocated more floorspace, meaning that Rolvenden School could now legally accommodate 189 pupils, rather than 232 as previously.

To the surprise of many, a ruling of the Education Department prevented the managers from using any of the trust funds of the Gybbon Charity. It all came down to the original wording of the trust deed back in 1707: because Gybbon only provided for the education of 'the poor,' without specifically mentioning a school, the authorities now felt the current school could not have access to such funds. It did not matter that the end result was the same, in that the village children were educated according to the founder's wishes – the money could no longer be regarded as an endowment of the school, and therefore the managers could not use it for their own purposes. Inevitably this caused more disappointment and resentment. As villagers began to wonder where the trust money was going, if not to their school, dark rumours began to circulate about the activities of the trustees.

Still the staff struggled on. To his surprise Mr Parker took delivery of a large quantity of medical inspection equipment. It turned out that he was now required to weigh and measure all the pupils himself; a pressing demand on his already heavy schedule. He was now teaching 70 of the eldest pupils in a classroom recognised to hold 50. In January 1910 Miss Close, Miss Morley and Miss Dinn all fell ill at the same time, and the village doctor advised the school to close for two weeks. The Kent Education Committee again refused to sanction the appointment of another teacher, and Miss Morley left to get married at the same time – leaving the school two staff members short. Eventually 19-year-old Miss Elsie Bayley, from Cranbrook but lately teaching at Harbledown near Canterbury, arrived in her place.

By now Miss Close had become engaged to a gentleman named Mr Brookes; a happy event tempered by the realisation that the school would probably lose her services, as with so many other young female teachers. But Mr Parker's log book entry for the week of 10th November 1910 records that she was absent, 'due to a bereavement.' Her fiancé had become seriously ill days earlier and, very shortly afterwards, he died. Ignorant of the reason why, the Kent Education Committee noted her absence, and demanded to know the reason for it from the managers – haughtily declaring that she would not be paid for her time away from work. The managers explained and made a strong representation that, under the circumstances, she should certainly be paid at the full rate. It would not be the last time they stood up for this much-respected teacher. This tragic event in Miss Close's life has given rise to some local folklore. She would never marry and, over sixty years later, the precious letters from her lost fiancé were found among her possessions after her death.

Not only were conditions uncomfortably cramped, but the very fabric of the school was falling apart as well. A medical inspection of in September 1910 made the following critical points:

> There are loose and broken tiles. The boys' urinal is untrapped and very foul. For 140 girls and infants there are only three closets. The pegs in the cloakroom are too close together. Some are broken and some missing. The ventilation of the mixed classroom is inefficient. The infants' room is insufficiently heated in winter.

In reply the managers sniffily asked whether the Medical Officer could 'see the managers on his visit, with a view to prevent additional correspondence on subjects already under consideration.' Nonetheless it was clear that money was needed more than ever, but very little was forthcoming from Rolvenden, as vicar Rev. Peter Drabble wrote in an appeal to the National Society:

We have only about seven residents in the parish who have the means to contribute to the cost of building the class room. The rest of the population consists of small farmers and hop-growers who have great difficulty in paying their way. If, moreover, we fail to comply with the order to supply the accommodation required it means the loss of our schools as non-provided [i.e. church school]*... I do hope that the National Society will give us substantial help. It would be a matter of deep regret, if after so many years spent in preserving the privileges of religious education at Brentford and Twickenham, I should have to give up that good cause.*

Rev. Peter Drabble, vicar of Rolvenden 1904-11.

The school's unlikely saviour was a solicitor, Michael Forbes Tweedie, who lived in London but had friends and family in Rolvenden. From what he heard, he felt sure that he could argue the school's case for the Gybbon trust funds being diverted to them. On 20th April 1911 he marched into the Whitehall office of the Board of Education and, without an appointment, demanded to speak to a representative. The hapless civil servant who listened to Tweedie's arguments could only note them down and send them to the Charity Commissioners for their comments. Two weeks later, the official approval was given for the school to receive the dividends that had accrued since they had stopped receiving them in 1904 – £182.11.3 in total – and a cheque duly arrived in the post. It was a remarkable and most unlikely turnaround, and Mr Tweedie was heartily thanked by the managers for his work, which he undertook free of charge.

In the summer of 1911 Bertha Goble resigned as monitress, and 21-year-old Miss Hilda Nutting, from Nonington near Canterbury, took her place as a supplementary teacher for the infants. At the same time Phoebe Dinn received her teaching certificate and left to teach in the mining village of Creswell, Derbyshire. She lived in Derbyshire for the rest of her life, and died there in 1967, aged 76. She stayed long enough in Rolvenden to enjoy the celebrations for the coronation of King George V in June, at which the school was closed for a week, and where the children received a mug and enjoyed a special tea and sports. Framed portraits of the new king and queen, to be prominently displayed in the school, were received from the Kent Education Committee shortly afterwards. Miss Clarice Young, 18 years old and from Ashford, replaced Miss Dinn in the Standard I class that October.

On 25th January 1912 the school was closed for pupils and staff to attend the official opening of the Church Room, a building which, to all intents and purposes, became the village hall and was later known as such. The villagers had donated generously towards it, and there was some concern among the managers that they would in consequence not be able to give as much to the school extension fund. In spite of this the people of Rolvenden again dug deep and building was able to begin between May and September, with the school forcibly closed for a month in the middle to accommodate the work.

The new Church Room, shortly after opening in 1912.

When the pupils returned in October the change was a revelation: a brand new classroom, new cloakrooms and refurbished lavatories for the boys. The total cost came in at £631, but thanks to the efforts of many — including Mrs Tennant of Great Maytham Hall who donated the proceeds of her fete (£81.6.1) towards it, and the staff who gave 35 shillings — it was paid off within months.

With more space the school could now comfortably accommodate 239 pupils; more or less exactly the number on its books. Hilda Nutting had since left to marry, becoming Mrs Turner, and her place in the infants' school was taken by 20-year-old Daisy Hook from Tenterden. The extra room allowed for the expansion of the school library — set up in the infants' room — and 150 new books were bought with the proceeds from a concert given by the pupils.

Possibly not unconnected to the improvement in conditions was a notable dip in the standard of behaviour at the school. In June 1913 eight boys were caught 'paddling and bathing in ponds in the dinner hour,' and a few months later churchwarden Horace Neve reported 'serious complaints' to the managers about the children's behaviour in the churchyard. In all cases the miscreants were punished, and steps taken to quell this streak of boisterousness. The Church of England Temperance Society visited regularly to lecture the older pupils on the evils of alcohol (which may or may not have been a factor), and the children were told to write essays on the subject.

1914 saw the loss of both Miss Hook, who went back to Smallhythe to teach, and Miss Bayley, who went on to teacher training at Goldsmith's College in London. In Miss Hook's place as supplementary teacher came 27-year-old Lily Swaffer, known as 'Cissy' and lately teaching with her sister May at Salehurst in Sussex. Their elder brother Alfred was a blacksmith who would, in time, set up at the forge in Rolvenden Layne. Cissy Swaffer was remembered by pupil Harry Millum 'by her hair pulled tight with a parting in the middle and a bun at the back, and her long boots buttoned to the knee.' Miss Bayley proved harder to replace, and the managers received no applications for her position. Miss Close's sister Katharine helped out for a week before it was decided that Mrs Parker would take on the duty – an arrangement that was supposed to be temporary but lasted for several years.

The upheaval coincided with high drama in Europe. Archduke Franz Ferdinand of Austria-Hungary was assassinated by a Serbian terrorist organisation on 28th June, which was used as an excuse by Germany to invade the Balkans. This set off a series of declarations of war, fed by a complex web of alliances that had caused Europe to be divided into two blocs: Germany, Austria-Hungary and Italy in one; Britain, France and Russia in the other. As German forces marched through Belgium in an attempt to encircle Paris, Britain – who had guaranteed Belgium's neutrality – declared war on 4th August.

Prior to the declaration of war, the school was closed on 22nd July to be used as a Red Cross hospital for wounded Belgian soldiers and sick refugees. This was later moved to the Church Room, but several boy scouts continued to help out rather than attending school. The managers complained about this, and in response the patients made a collection of £4.14.0 to the school which helped to calm things down. In time the Church Room would become an official Voluntary Aid Detachment hospital, with Grace Herring and Cissy Swaffer both volunteering as nurses. Mr Parker's sister Edith acted as quartermaster alongside Mrs Smith-Marriott, a charitable lady who set about providing large quantities of stockings and shoes for the poorest pupils to wear in bad weather. The schoolchildren were roped in to play 'patients' on whom the nurses could practise first aid – they were picked up from the school by horse-drawn cart and taken to a barn on the Tenterden road for the exercise.

VAD nurses practise first aid on children playing the roles of patients.

Belgian soldiers recovering in the Church Room.

The realities of the war soon became apparent. The Kent Educational Committee requested that each school formulate a plan to keep pupils safe from German air attacks – to which Rolvenden's rather flippant response was 'keeping the children as far as possible inside the buildings.' Later on they were to take advantage of a government scheme to insure the buildings against air-raid damage that never materialised. In February the school was closed for two days to provide billets for troops passing through the village on their way to the coast. As with any large-scale movement of people, illness became rife and the school routine was further disrupted by outbreaks of influenza, impetigo and chicken-pox. The Voluntary Training Corps was given the use of the schoolroom free of charge for their drilling, and several concerts and collections raised money for sympathetic causes, such as the relief of Belgian children. The annual Christmas treat was suspended during the war years, and the pupils instead sang carols to entertain the patients in the VAD hospital.

To make up for the shortage of labour, the authorities allowed children over 12 years of age to apply for licences to work on the land in the summer months rather than attend school. Later on the scheme was extended to children who needed to stay at home and look after younger siblings while their mothers went out to work. This was gratefully taken up by several parents and employers, though inevitably some tried to beat the system. In 1917 William Monk was refused a licence as his attendance was not good enough – he had already been working illegally. At the same time Harry Judge left his authorised employer – who regarded the boy as an unsatisfactory worker – and illegally went to work for another. By then, such was the situation with agriculture that the managers were compelled to grudgingly grant a new licence. As this decreased the school roll the pressure on the staff was lessened, and when Miss Young left in 1915 it was deemed unnecessary to replace her.

On the night of 22nd May 1917 the school was broken into, with 20 shillings stolen from Mr Parker's desk and 12 shillings from that of Miss Close. The culprit was never identified, and two months later the managers were shocked to receive a demand from the Kent Education Committee that Miss Close replace the amount stolen from her – which presumably had been earmarked for school purposes. The managers agreed to pass on the message, but warned the Committee that they would certainly support any protest Miss Close wished to make: as it happened, she referred the matter to the National Union of Teachers. The outcome is unknown, but it was another example – and not the last – of both the authorities' high-handed attitude towards Miss Close and the unwavering support she received from the school community. This support was much deserved: throughout the war years, she entered her pupils into competitions run by *St George's Magazine* to win prizes for their school. To Mr Parker's delight, they enjoyed at least eight successes with knitting, essay-writing and riddle-solving, and the school received many expensive and sought-after pictures as prizes. In addition, the teachers in Miss Close's family were always ready to step in as supply cover, as her brother Arthur did when Mr Parker was absent for a few days in July 1917.

The children were set to work foraging for supplies to help the war effort. In September 1917 they were asked to collect horse chestnuts by a mysterious notice which read 'This collection is invaluable war work and is very urgent. Please encourage it.' Over the next few weeks they collected nine hundredweight of conkers, receiving nine shillings and sixpence per hundredweight. Unbeknown to the children, they were sent to the Rock Brewery in Brighton for the extraction of acetone, a vital ingredient in the manufacture of cordite for explosives. The following autumn, by which time food rationing had been introduced, pupils were asked to go blackberry picking for the Government Jam Scheme, and the log book records that during October Rolvenden's children did so twice a week, under the supervision of Miss Close. In all, 353lbs of blackberries were gathered, but thanks to an administrative error in Maidstone they were not collected. Instead, Rolvenden's own village jam factory received the bulk of the fruit, and the pupils were rewarded with five pounds for their efforts – half of which was donated to the St Dunstan's Home for Blinded Soldiers.

A 1918 KEC certificate 'for regular attendance and good conduct.'

Of course, for some members of the school the war hit particularly close to home. Mr Parker's younger brother Herbert had been killed in France in May 1915. Miss Herring's brother Harold, serving in the Royal Navy, drowned in a submarine collision in the Firth of Forth in January 1918. Both Miss Close and Miss Swaffer also had brothers in uniform, all of whom mercifully survived. For a while it looked as though Mr Parker would be called up, and he attended a medical examination in Canterbury for the purpose – it took two worrying weeks before the confirmation that his job rendered him exempt. But the hardest thing for him, as with schoolteachers across the land, was coping with the deaths of men from Rolvenden he had either taught or been taught with as boys.

A glance at one of the war memorials today, either inside or outside of the church, shows that the village paid a particularly heavy price during the Great War. As there exists no list of pupils from the time, it is impossible to say definitively which of these men from Rolvenden attended the school as boys prior to their service. James Parker attempted to draw up a Roll of Honour of ex-pupils, both serving and fallen, but found it unfeasible. But many surnames are familiar to those who have called Rolvenden home, with some strongly linked to the school over several generations and into recent times: Beaney, Brunger, Bryant, Button, Cottingham, Elphee, Goble, Hayesmore, Hilder, Hyland, Judge, Maynard. It is a near-certainty that these, and others, were once boys who received their education in the classrooms of Rolvenden.

There was no rejoicing at the school when the Armistice was declared on 11th November 1918. The Spanish influenza pandemic, caused largely by the movement of soldiers, had spread through Rolvenden two weeks earlier and the school was closed. An attempt was made to open it on 18th November but several fresh cases caused it to close again for another week. Despite the wishes of all that 1919 would bring a clean slate, the consequences of the war would drag on for some time.

Chapter 6

INTO THE STORM

1919-38

THE HEADMASTER WAS uniquely committed to his charges, and tried to maintain a sense of permanence and stability while staff came and went; the result was that most children accepted such changes without question and certainly without their progress being impeded. Miss Herring left in June to become head of the infants' division at Lynsted in north Kent. She retired to Deal, where she died in 1944, aged 62. Her place at Rolvenden was taken by Kate Gilbert from Northamptonshire, rather older than her predecessors at 49, but with plenty of experience. Her father was Richard Gilbert, the celebrated head gardener of Burghley House, who invented several varieties of apples, melons and brassicas.

By coincidence, gardening was introduced to the boys' curriculum at about the same time, as well as cookery for the girls. This was a plan that had been mooted some years previously but interrupted by the war. Now that the Church Room was available, the girls' weekly classes began there in October 1920, taught by Mrs Armstrong, an itinerant cookery teacher from Biddenden. The boys began their gardening classes the following January, taught by Mr Parker himself, on a patch of land just behind. Large quantities of vegetables were grown and sold for school funds, and several boys in later

Boys in gardening (above) and girls in cookery (below) classes during the 1920s.

life remembered being taught how to 'double trench' and 'bastard trench' – the latter term provoking much sniggering.

The use of the Church Room as an extension of the school was deemed to be so satisfactory that another idea was pursued – that of establishing a canteen there for school dinners. Mr Parker argued that the experience of other schools had shown that a cooked lunch was beneficial to learning in the afternoon – let alone the social aspect of providing some of the poorest children with a decent meal. Unfortunately the plans fell through as a canteen was deemed not to be necessary, for the present. But as a compromise the children were given hot cocoa at lunchtime during the colder months.

One experiment that was sanctioned was a version of Daylight Saving Time in April 1921. During the lighter months, school was to begin at 9.30am rather than 9am, and all lessons began half an hour later than as stated on the timetable. But three weeks later Mr Parker reported to the managers that it had caused 'inconvenience to many,' and the plan was abandoned. During this spell, on 8th April, the children viewed a solar eclipse in the playground by casting shadows on to card.

The following year, Mrs Parker resigned her position through ill health, and Miss Florence Farrell came in on supply until 18-year-old Elsie Worthy, from Clapham, could be appointed for the autumn. However, the Kent Educational Committee got word that the number of pupils was nowhere near as large as at their peak ten years previously – the infants, in particular, had fallen from 51 pupils to just 20. They transferred Miss Swaffer to Ash, near Sandwich, and Miss Worthy was only allowed to stay one year before leaving for teacher training. Cissy Swaffer continued to teach but was compelled to retire after a botched operation rendered her disabled. She died in 1954, aged 68. Elsie Worthy gained her teaching certificate from Goldsmith's College and taught in several Kent schools. She retired to Ashford, where she died in 1980, aged 76.

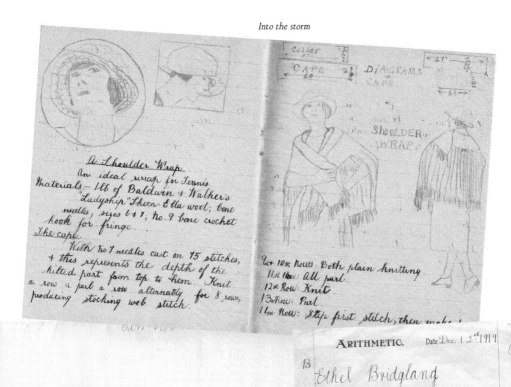

A Shoulder Wrap

An ideal wrap for Tennis.

Materials — 1lb of Baldwin & Walker's "Ladyship" Sheen-Ella wool; bone needles, sizes 6 & 7; No. 9 bone crochet hook for fringe.

The cape.

With no 7 needles cast on 75 stitches, & this represents the depth of the knitted part from top to hem. Knit a row & purl a row alternately for 8 rows, producing stocking web stitch.

9 & 10th Rows: Both plain knitting
11th Row: All purl.
12th Row: Knit.
13th Row: Purl.
14th Row: Slip first stitch, then make 1

The Blackberry

The Speedw

ARITHMETIC. Date Dec. 1 2ᵗʰ 1919.

Ethel Bridgland

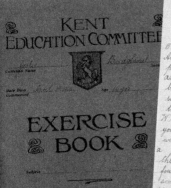

KENT EDUCATION COMMITTEE

EXERCISE BOOK

Subject —

May 13ᵗʰ 1921
Composition
A Day in my Holiday

One day I went to Tenterden with Auntie. We started about ten minutes past two o'clock. We walked quickly as we wanted to get at the bank before it closed. When we were coming down the town the church bells began to ring. When we got to the place where you go in to the church we saw a wedding. We stayed a quarter of an hour and then did the rest of our shopping. At about four o'clock we went and had some tea with auntie and uncle. We stayed there till a quarter to eight and then went home.

July 4ᵗʰ 1921
Composition
The Drought

The drought has lasted nearly three months now. The grass is very brown and dry looking. The hay is dry and so it can be cut one day and picked up the next day. The chicken go about with their mouths open and their wings hanging down below their bodies, although they have plenty of water. Hop gardens are very dry and the leaves are greenish yellow and some of the big leaves are brown. A lot of plants have hop flea on them. If no rain come the beans would not have the draught doth bin so bad as it would wash it off. The corn is yellow and will soon be ready to cut. Ponds are drying up, so we have to see that the animals have plenty to drink.

*A Standard I and II
class in the early 1920s.*

Throughout these uncertain times the horizons of the children began to widen. In common with other schools, there were holidays for the marriages of Princess Mary and the Duke of York (later King George VI). There was also a day off for the sombre dedication of Rolvenden's war memorial by the Archbishop of Canterbury in November 1922, at which Mr Parker led the choir. Empire Day in 1923 was marked by the distribution of a shellac disc of King George and Queen Mary's address 'to the boys and girls of the British Empire' and a gramophone was borrowed for the children to listen to it. One can imagine their wonder at hearing the monarch address them for the first time. On the same theme, Mr Parker recorded just weeks later that 'a motor-van showing animal and vegetable products of Canada stopped at the school this morning and the elder children were taken outside to see it.'

Into Miss Worthy's shoes stepped Daisy Smith, a dark-haired and lively 18-year-old from Headcorn. She played the piano for school singing, and immediately got on famously with Miss Close, with whom she shared a

Miss Daisy Smith.

passion for traditional country pursuits. Together they ran the Rolvenden Folk Dance Club which grew year on year, and the Junior Division took on such elements as sword-dancing and maypole dancing, to such traditional old routines as 'Rufty-Tufty' and 'Gathering Peascods.' Most recall Miss Smith as calm and sweet-natured; but even she had a limit. Kingsley Tester remembered that, when angry, 'she used to screw her eyes up into little slits and screech at you. It usually worked and things would carry on as normal.'

Miss Smith arrived just as a question mark was hanging over the infants' teacher Miss Gilbert. The managers' minutes record that the government inspector had advised that she be replaced by someone younger and with more modern teaching methods. However, the corresponding HMI report gives no such suggestion, and the only mention of the infants' class is that the room was inadequately heated. Whatever the circumstances, Miss

Gilbert was given notice and left in February 1924. Her replacement was 31-year-old Miss Edith Newman, born in Eastbourne and lately teaching at Petham, near Canterbury. She was forthright lady who brooked no nonsense, yet whose manner disguised a sweet and kindly nature that was most evident to those who behaved themselves. As with most teachers of this era, her pupils did not appreciate Miss Newman's more rounded personality until well after they left school.

The 1920s saw an increase in the activities of the NSPCC, particularly in rural districts, and an inspector was a fairly frequent visitor in these times to check on families reported to be neglecting their children. No prosecutions were made but it is certain that their very presence in the village improved the situations of certain pupils. Another visitor was the KEC medical inspector, who made special investigations into reports of badly nourished children. He was gratified to discover that there were 'remarkably few' in Rolvenden. But it is certainly true that conditions were primitive at the school, particularly with regard to sanitation, and it wasn't until after several years of wrangling that the premises were linked to mains drainage in 1927, the lavatories having been on the 'pail system' for 90 years. Word soon got around about this newfangled flushing apparatus, and over the next two summers tourists in charabancs who were visiting the church would cross the road to take advantage of the facilities. The managers instructed Mr Parker to put a stop to this practice.

The school in 1925, with staff in centre; (l-r) Edith Newman, James Parker, Daisy Smith and Daisy Close.

It is no surprise that outbreaks of illness still occurred – perhaps less frequently than in past times, but more potently when they did. Another bout of influenza swept through in February 1925, causing the school to be closed while it was disinfected from top to bottom. A little later, scarlet fever broke out, starting a well-established drill. Any siblings of the infected children still at school were sent home immediately, followed by those found to have peeling skin in a whole school inspection. The school was again closed to be disinfected, but the cases kept coming. So many pupils were kept at home through fear of infection that the only possible course was to close the school for three weeks. No sooner had scarlet fever been dealt with than measles broke out, and then diphtheria, and the cycle began again each time.

Tellingly, even Mr Parker — whose own record of service almost matched his father's — found his constitution weakened by the constant illness around him. He was compelled to take six weeks off in the winter of 1926-7, during which time the school was in the charge of a Mr W.H. Chase from the KEC supply pool. 60 years later, pupil George Button remembered how he used to 'sit with his feet on the desk smoking a pipe,' and was indifferent to the cheekier boys calling him 'Chaser.' He reminded them that he had 'long ears' — the better to hear their comments — to which the delighted boys responded with 'Donkey!' For all his light-heartedness, Mr Chase immediately identified an issue with the infants' class — that it was increasing in size and was already too big for just Miss Newman to handle. The managers agreed and on Mr Parker's return took on another temporary teacher, Mrs Margaret Gardner, to help out, with a view to making a permanent appointment in due course. The managers' eventual choice was Miss Evelyn Lamper, born near Arundel but teaching in Langton Green. Only 19 years old, the KEC had to approve her appointment, but her youth and vivacious energy helped to made her a success in her post. Thus the infants' school was divided in two: Miss Newman took the youngest children, and Miss Lamper the next class up, though the roles of each were swapped from time to time.

The unsatisfactory nature of the school buildings continued to tell. Newenden's school closed in 1929, and diocesan inspectors visited Rolvenden to see whether Newenden's children could be easily accommodated there, or whether they should pursue the other option of merging with Sandhurst Council School. Rolvenden would probably have been the best fit: there was little to compare in geographical distance, but it was closer to Newenden in ethos, both being church schools. But on seeing the facilities at Rolvenden the authorities decided to favour Sandhurst for the merger. It was a vote of little confidence that is reflected in other issues with the school fabric: electric light was considered by the managers but the idea was abandoned due to the expense; and during the winter of 1929 — the coldest of the century so far — it was found absolutely impossible to adequately heat the rooms. This caused Mr Parker to fall ill again, and his role was taken over by Miss Close for three days.

It was during the early 1930s that the efforts of the two Daisys — Close and Smith — really began to bear fruit, and folk activities at Rolvenden took off in a big way. A gramophone with which to teach folk-dancing was bought from the proceeds of several fundraising activities such as concerts held at the Church Room. The two doughty teachers gained permission to take most of August 1930 off to attend a Summer School at Folkestone which gave them the means to enter teams from the school into the English Folk Society's junior competitions in song and dance. Rolvenden always excelled at these events, placing very highly in both disciplines, and proved particularly strong at sword-dancing. The infants had a counterpart in Miss Lamper, who accompanied pupils to competitions in harmony singing, usually held at Tunbridge Wells.

The school's Folk Dance Society, circa 1930.

The supply teacher who covered for the absence of Misses Close and Smith in August 1930 was an ex-pupil of the school, Miss Evelyn Hinds. Originally from West Cross, she had been marked out as a promising student and gained a junior scholarship to attend the Ashford County School for Girls in June 1914, aged twelve. She then trained as a teacher and worked in schools all over the world: France, Italy, Norway, Canada, Australia and New Zealand. When she returned to Rolvenden for a few weeks' work it seems precious little teaching was done, but a lot of learning nonetheless, as she regaled her pupils with stories of her many adventures. Afterwards she took up appointments at Dymchurch and then as headteacher of Newchurch School, during which time she saw out the war years – while the military authorities made use of the photographs she had taken of the Norway coast. She became an author of some note, writing thriller novels and memoirs of her travels. She emigrated to Canada where she was invested a Member of the Order of Canada, and died there in 1991, aged 89.

It was becoming clear that Mr Parker's health was beginning to fail him: he spent three months of early 1931 off sick, and for the second time an outside headteacher from the supply pool was brought in to take charge. He was Captain Charles Quin, remembered as militaristic and disciplined, who after Rolvenden would go on to become the headmaster of Pluckley School. It was recalled that he often put boys to work washing his car, taught them how to box, and to march in a disciplined fashion (and without hesitation) into the traffic when crossing the road. The KEC put Mr Parker on half pay during his illness, though there was a special request from the school managers that his case be treated as generously as possible.

*In February 1931, unfortunately coinciding with Mr
Parker's absence, official photographs were taken of each
class. These were later sold as postcards to parents.*

*Left: Miss Lamper (lower infants); Miss Newman (upper
infants); Miss Smith (Standards I and II).*

*Above: Miss Close (Standard III); Captain Quin
(Standards V-VII).*

Mr Parker's return to work in April coincided with a period of some turmoil. Miss Newman, who had been suffering ongoing back problems caused by a fall the previous year, was found to require an operation which would mean a month off work. This turned out to be six months, and supply teacher Miss Ellen Hussey was appointed to teach her infants' class in the meantime. In January 1932 two severe accidents (concussion with a badly cut forehead, and a broken leg) occurred to pupils on the same day. That same month Miss Close was accused of the 'unsympathetic treatment' of a pupil who was ill enough to be admitted to a London hospital – once again, the school managers expressed their support of her and complete confidence in her actions. Then in March she was the victim of theft for a second time, when 13-year-old Thomas Newick broke into the school and took eight shillings from a tin belonging to the Folk Dance Club. He was sent to an industrial school for three years by the magistrates.

These trials appear to have been the final straw for Mr Parker's constitution. Wednesday 15th June was his last day in charge of Rolvenden School: he was taken ill the next day, giving way to Miss Close initially and then, for the third time, a supply headteacher came on board. William Overton from Reading was given the nickname 'Mr Ovaltine' – also rather ironically, as a scheme to distribute a warm mug of Horlicks at morning break (3d a week, taken up by 80 pupils) had just begun. It is recalled that the defining feature of these summer months of 1932 was the amount of outdoor learning instigated by the headmaster. Any excuse was taken to get out of the confines of the classroom; either on a daily nature walk, or map survey work as far off as Benenden and Iden Green. These advanced notions were viewed with suspicion by some parents, but thoroughly enjoyed by their children.

The managers once again lobbied the KEC for 'favourable consideration' towards James Parker and his salary, but matters were decided for them when the stricken headteacher submitted his resignation in October. Mr Overton was to continue until Christmas; but he would be doing so without Miss Smith, who left in November. As farewell gifts she received 'a set of silver napkin rings, a silver toast rack and a cut-glass sugar dredger with silver top.' She was also presented with a gramophone record case and money to buy further records; a legacy of her work with the Folk Dance Club. Laden down with generosity and good wishes, she sailed to India to marry her fiancé, becoming Mrs Cecil Hole. The couple later returned to her home in Headcorn where she died in 1982, aged 77.

Having retired, James Parker's health rallied to an extent – probably suggesting that his complaint could have been due to the nature of his work. His had enough energy to build his family a home, Passfield, just a couple of doors down from his beloved school. For the next few years he was a regular sight in the village, sometimes in a wheelchair, exchanging a friendly word to his old pupils – even if he did still insist they doff their caps in greeting. He was less regularly seen after the tragic loss of his youngest son Philip, serving as a corporal in the RAF, who was killed when his aircraft crashed in Scotland in April 1937.

James Parker died on 8th January 1940, four decades to the day since the death of his father Francis. His funeral repeated the same scenes, forty years on, and the village virtually shut down as scores of friends, relatives and pupils crammed into the church. His obituary related that 'his services were never sought in vain and his sympathetic and kindly disposition endeared him to all,' and that he would be remembered 'with affection and esteem by hundreds of school children.' That is surely an understatement. He was the last of an unbroken family line that educated Rolvenden's children for a century and a half, and his end was also the end of an era. It would take a particularly special man to follow it.

ROLVENDEN DOMINIE'S RETIREMENT.

MR. JAMES PARKER'S LONG ASSOCIATION WITH CHURCH SCHOOL.

The last day of the summer term, which is normally a time of great rejoicing, was this year tinged with sadness for the boys and girls of Rolvenden Church School. For on that day they bade farewell to their Headmaster, Mr. James Parker, who for more than 30 years has been the guide, philosopher and friend of Rolvenden's young people.

ROLVENDEN HEAD RETIRES.

Family's Record Broken After Nearly A Century.

After nearly 33 years' service, Mr. James Parker has resigned his appointment as headmaster, of Church of England School, Rolvenden, owing to ill-health.

He succeeded his father as headmaster.

In ter in 1900, after Par† the latter had held den the post for 37 years, Brit and his mother's as father, the late James Oxley, previously headmaster there for a long period.

Mr. Parker is the son of the late Mr. F. W. Parker, and was born in School House. In his early days he was a pupil teacher at Bethersden, afterwards being transferred to Ashford. After several years at college he served as assistant master at Holy Trinity, Eastbourne, for three years. He then succeeded his father at Rolvenden School.

Happy relations have always existed between him and his pupils. He remarked in conversation with a "Kent Messenger" representative that the school was enlarged in 1912, and at that time there was 230 children on the register. Now there were only 150, the decrease he thought being caused partly through the war, and the fact that large families were no longer customary.

LOCAL WORK.

Mr. Parker was for 31 years Clerk to the Parish Council, and Assistant Overseer for 27 years. He has been hon. secretary to the local branch of the Conservative Association for 27 years. He is still people's warden, hon. secretary to the Church Council and Church Room Committee.

Mrs. Parker is associated with the Infant Welfare Centre, and for several years took an active part in the work of the Women's Institute. During the war she assisted teaching in school.

Mr. and Mrs. Parker are hoping to spend their retirement in a house adjacent to the school, which they are having built.

MR. J. PARKER.

MR. J. PARKER

ROLVENDEN LOSES A NOTED PERSONALITY

All Rolvenden is bereaved by the death of Mr. James Parker, which occurred at his residence, Passfield, on Monday.

Born at School House, Rolvenden, Mr. Parker, who was 66 years of age, had been closely identified with the educational work and parochial and social activities of the village for almost the whole of his life. He succeeded his father as head master of the Church of England School some 40 years ago, and held that position for 32 years, retiring in 1932. He then took up his residence at "Passfield." He held many local appointments of which a great number were of a voluntary character. For many years he was clerk to the Parish Council and was also rate collector. He was secretary to the Church Room from the time of its opening until quite recently; for a long time choirmaster and a member of the church choir; secretary to the Rolvenden Non-Ecclesiastical Charities, the Conservative Association, the National Savings' Association. His other local activities have included that of churchwarden and secretary of the Parochial Church Council. In fact there was hardly a phase of the village life in which Mr. Parker had not taken an active part, while his influence for the welfare of the community was far reaching.

His services were never sought in vain and his sympathetic and kindly disposition endeared him to all: Mr. Parker had been in ill-health for some years.

It is a coincidence that his death occurred on the same day of the week and almost the same hour as that of his father 40 years ago. He leaves a widow and three sons. Mr. Parker's youngest son, Corporal Philip Parker, R.A.F., was killed in an air crash in April, 1937.

The funeral will take place this (Friday) afternoon at 2 p.m.

ROLVENDEN

BELOVED SCHOOLMASTER'S DEATH.

Mr. James Parker, who will be remembered with affection and esteem by hundreds of school children, passed away at Passfield on Monday. Mr. Parker, who was schoolmaster for 32 years, retired some seven years ago owing to ill-health. Until his health became impaired Mr. Parker was actively associated with practically all the village organisations, and held a number of public appointments. He was formerly rate collector, Clerk to the Parish Council, secretary of the Conservative Association, secretary of the Parochial Church Council, choirmaster and chu~ ~warden. Much sympathy will be ext~ ~dow and three sons in the

ROLVENDEN

THE LATE MR. J. PARKER—The funeral took place on Friday, following a service conducted by the Rev. H. B. Langton, of Mr. James Parker, formerly schoolmaster for 32 years, whose death was reported last week. The immediate mourners included Mrs. Parker, Mr. James Parker, Mr. A. D. Parker, Mr. S. Parker, Mrs. A. D. Parker, Miss M. Parker, Miss Parker, Mr. and Mrs. F. W. Parker, Mr. R. S. Parker, Mr. and Mrs. J. Toop, Mr. and Mrs. G. Young, Mr. and Mrs. H. Burden, Mr. Burden, jun. The Weald of Kent Lodge of Freemasons was represented by Mr. C. A. Whitehead, Mr. H. L. Caryer, Mr. A. Hilder, Mr. J. Barman, Mr. P. S. Stone, Mr. H. J. Allsop, Mr. H. P. Stone and Mr. S. Rutherford. The Weald of Kent Association Teachers and Teachers' Provident Society was represented by Mr. E. Boulding. Others present included Mrs. H. J. Tennant, Mr. Horace Neve, Mrs. H. B. Longton, Mrs. Piper, Mr. J. A. Bathurst, Mr. Wilcocks, Miss Close, Miss Gillman, Miss A. N. Dann, Mr. F. Burden, Mrs. Burden, Miss E. Parker, Mr. G. H. Baker, Mr. F. Morfee, Mr. H. W. Hoad, Mrs. Button, Mr. Terry, Mrs. G. N. Taylor, Mr. C. T. Stapley, Mrs. Inge and Mr. Polle.

That man was **Percy Langley Willcocks**, though in deference to the fact that he hated his given name, he was known to all as John. He was born in London in 1900, attended the Judd School in Tonbridge, and served as an air officer at the very end of the First World War. He married Florence (known as Susan) Seagars at Lynsted in 1926, served as headmaster at the village of Boxley, north of Maidstone, and welcomed daughter Joy and son Pat. He took up his new position in Rolvenden at the start of 1933, with another daughter, Annette, arriving later that year.

Mr Willcocks was a cultured and artistic man who continued his predecessors' love of music and was active in the performing arts. He identified the need for a new piano, and persuaded the managers to act as guarantors to a loan for it, assuring them that the payments would be covered by the takings from school concerts. (The sale of hot cocoa to the children raised five pounds towards the objective in the

Mr and Mrs Willcocks, with children (l-r) Joy, Annette and Pat, at School House, 1934.

first few months.) Whole school singing was started, last thing on a Friday afternoon, and before long the singers were of a good enough standard to give several well-received performances. Mr Willcocks also had a taste for the rhetoric style of teaching he had enjoyed at grammar school. Gone were the stuffy monochrome books, and in came colourful stories. He encouraged class debates; two discussion topics being 'The wireless will mean the end of the gramophone' and 'What will England do when we are no longer the workshop of the world, as other countries learn how to make their own goods?' This style was more akin to university than an elementary school, and perhaps also reflected the fact that, while at Rolvenden, Mr Willcocks was studying for a London economics degree in his spare time.

Sword-dancing boys, circa 1933.

Starting at the same time as the new headmaster was Thelma Sole, who immediately struck up a firm friendship with Miss Lamper, and when the latter left the profession to marry in October 1933, Miss Sole acted as her bridesmaid. Miss Lamper became Mrs Doubleday and later married into the Britcher family, remaining in Kent for the rest of her life. She died in 1997, aged 90.

The new staff entered a school that was traditional, which suited them, and old-fashioned to the point of crumbling, which did not. A complicating factor was that there was now a small element of competition from St David's School, run by Miss Clegg on the Tenterden road just outside the village centre. This private enterprise was modest, consisting of no more than a dozen pupils, but it throw into focus some inadequacies of the much larger village school.

By 1935 it was an increasing concern that the school buildings required a lot of investment to bring them up to scratch. There had been continual reports for many years about draughts, leaking roofs, cracks in walls and plaster falling from ceilings. The infants' room was notoriously impossible to heat effectively, the lavatories disgusting and the playground surface dangerous, and in addition several important repairs were necessary to the school house. But the managers' hands were stayed by the prospect of a new 'central school' at Tenterden being proposed by Kent County Council. This school – which would eventually become Homewood – was envisaged to replace the upper years of all surrounding village schools, though at this point no-one knew at which age the pupils would be transferred. Understandably, the managers did not want to risk spending money on the repair of a school that was expected to become part-redundant, and the matter was allowed to slide.

Parades on Empire Day,
1935.

Infants, 1936.

Middle class, 1936.

Senior class, 1936.

Into the storm

Folk dancers, 1936.

*Rounders team,
1936.*

Cricket team, 1936.

R.J. Unstead became a widely-read author of children's history books.

Just before the school broke up for the summer holidays in August 1936, Mr Willcocks was absent for a week. His position was covered by a newly-qualified teacher from Ramsgate, Robert Unstead, who 20 years later as R.J. Unstead would become the author of a celebrated series of illustrated history books for schoolchildren. Titles such as *People in History* and *The Story of Britain* gave a clear and accessible narrative, and were a fixture of primary school history classes all over the country for many years. Mr Willcocks would certainly have approved.

The remarkable year of 1936 also marked the peak of the wireless broadcast, with the BBC providing a special schools' programme. In October this was received at Rolvenden for the first time in the upper class, and proved so successful that it was extended to the whole school. A few weeks later, Mr Willcocks noted that the school listened to the Remembrance Day broadcast from Whitehall. Shortly afterwards, the abdication of Edward VIII would be observed by Mr Willcocks from his sick-bed – an illness developed into influenza, and he didn't return to school until February. By this time Phyllis Swan had joined to help Miss Newman with the infants. The variation in pupil numbers over time was so great that the position hadn't needed to be filled since Miss Lamper left over three years previously.

The 1937 cricket team were champions of the Weald of Kent Schools Sports Association.

The managers met in March 1937 to discuss a series of complaints (by persons unknown) about the 'unsanitary condition' of the lavatories. It was decided to look into their complete reconstruction, and an estimate for the work was received at £120 – an amount well out of reach. The issue of the central school at Tenterden again raised its head, with a likely opening projected for 1939. The managers again decided that they could not justify raising and spending such a large sum until they were in a position to know just how many pupils they would be expected to accommodate. Therefore no action was taken. Then in December a routine health inspection precipitated a real crisis. The Medical Officer, Dr Galbraith, took one look at the lavatories, and the condition of the buildings generally, and officially condemned them as unfit for use. Claims were made in a meeting of the Tenterden Rural District Council – the body responsible for health and sanitation issues – that 'nothing had been done' on the part of the managers. They were quick to repudiate these claims, arguing that their reasoning had been sound.

In the midst of this crisis Phyllis Swan left the school's employment to marry a Sri Lankan gentleman, becoming Mrs Sinnappu Rajaratnam. Inevitably, in 1930s rural Kent, this raised some eyebrows – but not, if must be said, among the staff and pupils of the school, who were delighted at her frequent return visits to many old friends. She settled in Teddington, West London, and died in 1986, aged 71. Thelma Sole left shortly afterwards, settling near Canterbury and becoming Mrs John Birt. She died in 2008 at the grand age of 97. Her replacement Miss Hickman stayed only a few months before giving way to Miss Brooks, who would also leave after just under a year.

Daisy Close (centre) with Phyllis and Sinnappu Rajaratnam.

It was a torrid and uncertain time behind the scenes at the school, as in the world at large. Desperate efforts were made to seek out potential sources of money to improve matters and make up for exactly one hundred years of underfunding. One by one they drew blanks, and with every inspection by a new official the list grew: a proper heating system; electric lighting; damp-proofing; repairs to the roof. By July the writing was on the (damp and crumbling) wall – Rolvenden School could no longer continue as a self-supporting school under the voluntary auspices of the church. A suggestion to make an appeal to the villagers was dismissed as a waste of time, based on a previous 'entire lack of response.' Reluctantly, the managers agreed to begin the process of handing the school over to Kent County Council, thus becoming the 'council school' – the successor to the old 'board school' – that many had fought so hard over the years to avoid. The application for a council takeover was approved, and Rolvenden School became a council school on 14th November 1938, losing 'Church of England' from its official title.

To most people the routine continued as normal, and the pupils noticed very little difference, if any. The entire staff – Mr Willcocks, Miss Close, Miss Newman and Miss Brooks – were dismissed and reappointed in the blink of an eye, becoming council employees in a legal instant. But it must have been particularly galling for the vicar, Rev. Hugh Langton, who had diligently and reverently supported the school since his arrival in 1928, visiting every week to give religious instruction, take prayers, and lead an assembly in the church – his black clerical garb gaining him the rather uncharitable nickname of 'The Rook.' Now he was cast off, his good work ended, and no longer a school manager by virtue of his position as vicar. But this was no reflection on his role – it all came down, simply, to lack of money. And the children were still obliged to take religious studies as part of a rounded education – the rule was now that it could not be just of an Anglican character. After 101 years as a church school, and quite clearly struggling in latter years, it was the only course left open.

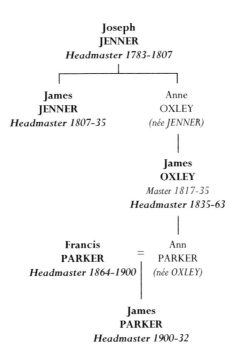

The five-generation teaching dynasty that led Rolvenden School for 149 years, 1783-1932.

ROLVENDEN
C. P. School.
1950

Chapter 7

A COUNTY SCHOOL

1939-62

THERE IS NO doubt that, by coming under Kent County Council control, what Rolvenden School lost in autonomy it gained in resources. Suddenly a wave of officials descended, assessing requirements, drawing up plans and budgeting for the work. All this activity was halted with the coming of another war. The signs had been there for some time: despite Chamberlain's promise of 'peace for our time' just a week earlier, the girls' domestic science class had been disrupted in October 1938 by the occupation of the Church Room for Air Raid Precaution training. The following April, the managers discussed plans for emergency conditions in the event of war being declared. 705 evacuees were expected in Rolvenden, of which between 400 and 500 would be of school age and would require space in which to be taught. In a school already struggling with space for its own children, this seemed an impossible task. Even the sizeable School House was now overcrowded: the Willcocks family took on five extra children – four from the same family, and another who had moved from his original billet in Stone-in-Oxney.

Yet the spirit of the times prevailed. On 19th September 1939 the school reopened early for the newly-arrived evacuees. They were accompanied by

13 teachers – three men and ten women – and came from an area roughly south of Catford and north of Bromley, with pupils mostly from Rangefield or Churchdown Schools. The evacuees and home pupils were all grouped together, irrespective of school, and told to attend classes according to where they lived or were billeted in the parish. A circle was drawn on a map radiating out from the school by eight-tenths of a mile – the distance, as the crow flies, to the Ewe and Lamb at Rolvenden Layne. Any pupil who lived inside the resulting circle would be grouped separately to those who lived outside. One group would go to classes at the school in the morning while the other group attended an informal 'meeting' (infants in the Church Room; older children in the Club House) consisting of recreational activities and games; then, after lunch, the groups would swap over. In the midst of this, trainee teacher Angela Edmonds arrived for several weeks' experience, which must have been atypical to say the least.

As the months passed in this 'Phoney War,' which saw little or no enemy action at home, there was plenty of time for fun. Showbusiness couple Jean Stirling Mackinlay and Harcourt Williams – theatre stalwarts at London's Old Vic, but living in Reading Street near Tenterden – turned up at the Church Room to give the schoolchildren a concert of folk singing. A special programme of entertainment in the school was drawn up for the evacuees over Christmas – though the prospect of spending the season away from home proved too much for both children and parents, and many were recalled to London.

The war came home suddenly in May 1940 with the German advance through the Low Countries and France, leading to the evacuation of Allied forces from Dunkirk. As the Luftwaffe fought for air supremacy over the Royal Air Force – the first objective of the planned invasion – the people of Kent were front-line witnesses to the Battle of Britain raging above their heads. On 25th July an air-raid began at 2.45pm, compelling all children to be kept inside, and the all-clear was not sounded until well after school hours. Owing to difficulties in getting them home safely, some were not able to leave the site until 7.30pm, by which time the staff had been sorely tested in keeping them occupied. This happened several times at the height of the air battle in July and August, and severe disruption to the school routine became commonplace. In September the side of the Club House used for activities was damaged by a stray bomb. When school began again in October, the pupils there had to assemble around the billiard table on the other side of the building until the damage was repaired.

The Kent War Agricultural Committee ('War Ag'), responsible for supporting farm production, built a concrete block and corrugated iron building on the Hook family's land to the immediate rear of the school playground. In here was stored mostly agricultural machinery and vehicles that were rented out to local farms to help improve their efficiency. The pupils were fascinated by the working of such machines so close to their boundary, and spent happy hours watching the labourers come and go – many of whom were relatives. At other times the building became an extension to the playground itself, with children shinning up the walls and clambering over the roof, or using it for target practice with snowballs in winter.

Miss Jones was appointed in 1941 as an unhurried replacement for Miss Brooks. When winter came and the nights grew longer, the start of the school day was put back to 9.30am thanks to difficulties in negotiating travel during the blackout. Though the government promised a brick air-raid shelter for every school, demand was so intense that one was not provided until halfway through the conflict. (Previous to this, children had been instructed to get under their desks with their heads close to the floor.) Ironically, the air-raid shelter was the only part of the school to enjoy electric lighting. At the Church Room, the soldiers billeted in the village laid on parties for the children, and a warming bowl of midday soup was provided to pupils who wished it from February 1942. This idea, brought about in a time of strict rationing, was so successful that the canteen idea was reconsidered. By August it was confirmed: from January 1943, a canteen would be established in the Church Room for midday lunches. The food was to be prepared at a Central Cooking Depot at Cranbrook, and distributed to participating schools in large metal canisters. The new arrangement began on 25th January and soon proved its worth, with most pupils joining the scheme.

Food waste was strictly controlled, with the best leftovers being redistributed and the rest diverted to animal feed. The children were regularly given strong messages of the 'waste not want not' variety, such as with a scrap salvage drive run by Lady Geddes – wife of Auckland Campbell Geddes, the Commissioner for Civil Defence in the southeast region – who lived at Frensham Manor in the Layne. An essay competition run by Tenterden Rural District Council in connection with Wings for Victory week was won by pupil Derek Hunnisett, whose work was described as 'outstandingly the best.' Then a book salvage drive collected thousands of books for either redistribution into the Forces or recycling into paper which was in very short supply.

The senior class, circa 1944.

Sparkeswood House had been taken over as a Public Assistance home for 35 disadvantaged evacuees from London, all of infant school age. Enquiries were made about accommodating them in the infants' room at the school, but the already cramped conditions seemed to make this impossible. Nonetheless a compromise was reached: in January 1943 the eldest of the Sparkeswood children were admitted to the school. Then in June Miss Newman's class of the youngest 'home' infants was transferred to Sparkeswood, which for the remainder of the war became an extension of Rolvenden School for the smallest pupils. There was a happy consequence for the Willcocks family, who became particularly close to one of the Sparkeswood boys and adopted him as their own, renaming him John – a second son to the family.

In the aftermath of the D-Day landings in June 1944, when the war went back the way it had come, a new terror was unleashed on Kent – the V-1 flying bomb, or 'doodlebug.' Trained on London, these often fell short or were shot down by the RAF, meaning that more actually landed in Kent than on their intended target of London. In fact, the district of Tenterden (which includes Rolvenden) suffered more V-1 hits than any other – 238, with Ashford a distant second at 189. They were first sighted on 13th June, and the government hurriedly drew up plans for the wholescale evacuation of children from the southeast to further north and west – generally, the opposite direction to 1939. Registration for Rolvenden's children to be evacuated began on 15th July, and the first group of nine children travelled to Somerset three days later, accompanied by Mr Willcocks. Many parents resisted at first, but minds were soon changed, for on the day after that first evacuation – 19th July – Rolvenden suffered its only civilian casualties of the war. A flying bomb landed at Little Pookwell Farm, in the west of the parish, obliterating a house and killing 38-year-old Alice Winter and her 13-year-old daughter Violet. While she had been a pupil at nearby Sandhurst, the loss of the Winters was keenly felt by many Rolvenden families who knew them personally. On the day of their deaths, the Sparkeswood children were travelling to Yorkshire with Miss Newman, and by the end of July the school roll of 155 had fallen to 79 pupils present.

It was a wise choice for many. On 30th July the school bore the brunt of an explosion when a doodlebug dropped in a nearby field. Most of the windows were blown in and ceiling-plaster crashed down on to the desks below. Mercifully, it was a Sunday and nobody was present, otherwise there would certainly have been casualties. The flying bombs arrived without warning, other than their characteristic drone, and there was rarely time to take cover. Even if they passed over, there was the frequent threat of being caught in the machine-gun fire of RAF fighters trying to bring them down. One night this summer, School House was hit by a British cannon shell which narrowly missed the Willcocks' sleeping son Pat, passing through his mattress. It left a hole in the side of the wall, which the headmaster demonstrated to his pupils in the playground by poking a stick through it and waving to them from inside the house.

Miss Close, now aged 65, retired at the end of the 'doodlebug' summer after 38 years serving the school. At her farewell gathering she was presented with a cheque for £34 15s, and a beautifully made book, hand-bound and lettered by Mr Willcocks, containing the names of all 260 subscribers to the fund. Rev. Langton paid tribute to her 'faithful and efficient service' and added some remarks which could well have applied to several other members of staff over the years:

> *[38 years is] a very long slice of anyone's life and to be able to look back on it as having been spent in the service of others must be to her a thankful remembrance and a cause of gratitude to all to whom she has given that service.*

Daisy Close spent much of the rest of her life in the bungalow she had had built adjacent to James Parker's old house. She was a regular visitor to the school, just a short walk away, and her visits were always received with eagerness. When she died in May 1974, aged 94, the many hundreds of pupils she had taught were able to reflect that this lady, the product of a bygone era and a genuine link with the past, had truly given her life to Rolvenden.

19⁰⁶44

A TOKEN
REMINDER

Mr. J. Addy....
Mr. H. J. Allsop.
Mrs. Archbald..
Mrs. Atkinson.
Mrs. Attfield..
Mrs. A. Austen.
Mr. G. Austen.
Mrs. Baker....
Edie & Edward...
.......Baker.
Col. Barham...
Mr. H. A. Barham

The village teacher everyone loved dies

A LONG chapter of service to Rolvenden, which lasted almost 70 years, has been ended by the death of Miss Daisy Ellen Close.

She died in her sleep at Vest View Hospital, 'enterden, last Thursay. She was 94. Almost everyone in the illage knew her and a onsiderable proportion of the adult population had received the benefit of her kindly advice when she taught at the local school for nearly 40 years.

What perhaps not' so many know is that it was through misfortune that she remained for so long. In 1911 the young fellow teacher to whom she was engaged died. But for that tragedy she would almost certainly have married and moved away.

As it was she continued teaching until 1944 and then began what proved to be a long and active retirement.

Among the jobs she had undertaken in the village were church council secretary, secretary and treasurer of the Church Room committee, founder member and treasurer of the Gardening Society, secretary of the Gibbons Educational Trust, Guide captain, National Savings collector, a founder member of the Women's Institute, and a helper with the infant welfare clinic.

Miss Close had to go into hospital more than two years ago, but was able to make occasional visits to the village and her former bungalow home where she had been looked after for so long by another teacher, Miss Kathleen Brown.

She remained active to the end, spending her time knitting for Oxfam, her favourite charity, and writing her memories of life in the village.

Cremation was at Charing yesterday. A memorial service is to be held at Rolvenden Parish Church on Sunday, June 9, at 6.30 p.m. The address is to be given by Wing Commander A. H. Button, of Littlestone, one of her former pupils.

The middle class, circa 1945.

It was harder to replace Miss Close than anyone had imagined, there being not a single application for the vacancy. In the end Miss Day was seconded from Benenden to be in temporary charge of the infants, with Miss Jones taking the lower and Mr Willcocks the upper juniors. This was manageable while half the pupils remained in safer parts of the country, but on their return in December – the V-1 threat having passed – things became crowded and unmanageable. Perhaps not unconnected was an episode a few weeks later when a group of older boys broke into the War Ag building, vandalising several cars by putting sugar in the petrol tanks. Nine boys were summoned to appear before the Cranbrook magistrates on 14th March, where they were given stern reprimands from the bench.

When peace came to Europe in May 1945 it was marked at the school with two days' holiday. The end of the war would have allowed the scheme of improvements to be picked up again, except that almost immediately, a debate started on whether to extend the school on the current site, on another site, or to abandon it and build a new school elsewhere. With the coming baby boom – the increase in the birth-rate precipitated by the return of soldiers after the war – it was expected that the school roll would peak in the early 1950s, and action needed to be taken to increase room. Opinions flew back and forth for several years: to add new classrooms to the Falstaff field (behind the current motor museum); to continue using Sparkeswood House and convert it properly; to build a new school behind the Church Room? All the time discussions continued the most pressing matters – such as installing electric light – were deferred again and again.

Conditions remained hard for several years after the war. During the particularly harsh winter of 1946-7 the water pipes frosted up and the supply of coal ran out. Water had to be carried over from School House, and coal was borrowed from the villagers' own supplies for over a week. As food rationing continued, the school was asked to effect a 10% reduction in numbers using the canteen, and all the children (except those under six and those coming from a distance) went without a hot meal once a fortnight.

Thus Rolvenden, like the rest of the country, muddled through on the narrowest of margins. Into these straightened post-war times arrived Roger, a fifth child for Mr Willcocks, thus completing their family.

The shortages and upheavals were reflected in the staff. Miss Jones left the profession to get married, Miss Day returned to Benenden, and a succession of teachers were brought in from other

The 1946-7 football team.

schools as supernumerary staff: Mr Dowsett, Mr Emberton and Mr Skellet were three short-term examples. The Sparkeswood arrangement was wound up, and Miss Newman returned to the main site, but health concerns forced her to go part-time. Taking her place with the infants was Miss Ryan from Widnes, remembered as a glamorous lady with long, painted nails. But rustic Rolvenden proved too much of a culture shock, and she resigned after only a few months. The replacements for Miss Jones and Miss Ryan were far more enduring, becoming two of the school's longest-serving and best-loved members of staff. Kathleen Brown from Worcester was a caring lady who pulled off the delicate trick of being firm and gentle at the same time. She became a familiar sight in the area on her old bicycle, and became particularly fond of Miss Close, with whom she moved in and became a live-in carer. Bessie Elliott (née Britcher) was an ex-pupil whose family hailed from the Layne, and had married husband Ken, himself a teacher, just prior to taking up the position at her old school. She was a good friend of Joan Edmonds, married to ex-pupil John, who arrived at the same time in place of Miss Day.

The staffing was now as follows: the infants with Mrs Elliott (and occasionally Miss Newman), then the lower juniors with Miss Brown, the middle class with Mrs Edmonds and the oldest pupils with Mr Willcocks. This period of stability, remembered by many as something of a golden age, would not last more than a few months. Homewood School was due to open in October 1949, with all 13-14 years olds transferred immediately, and the 11-12 year olds at the start of 1950. In advance of this, the managers were set the task of reorganising Rolvenden School, given that the roll would drop by over a third, to around 80 pupils. A school of this size would only require a headteacher and two assistant teachers, so one member of staff would have to go.

Mrs Elliott, specialising in the teaching of infants, was regarded as safe. Neither Miss Brown nor Mrs Edmonds wished to leave Rolvenden voluntarily. Mr Willcocks also expected to stay on but, privately, the managers had their reservations. For one, it was generally agreed that his teaching style was most suited to pupils over the age of 11, and his talents would therefore be better employed in a secondary school. Secondly, it was rather cynically suggested that a female headteacher would be cheaper to employ, and more appropriate in covering the classes of younger pupils when Mrs Edmonds or Mrs Elliott – both of whom were recently married – took time off to start their own families. The managers therefore decided to recommend a headmistress to Kent County Council. Showing immense good grace, Mr Willcocks accepted this decision, but it was overruled by the Education Committee, who pointed out that there was a shortage of female teachers and professed their confidence in him to make things work.

Thus began an uncomfortable stand-off with the managers, who felt duty bound to hold their position, especially as it now looked as though the axe would be swung in the direction of the oldest teacher: they stated formally that they did not wish 'to be associated with any decision to terminate the appointment of Miss Brown.' Events resolved themselves by two pieces of good timing. At the time of Homewood's opening, Miss Brown was seconded to Wittersham – where the school had the opposite problem, of being understaffed. By the time of her return nine months later, Mrs Edmonds had resigned to have her first child. Miss Brown was neatly reinstated at Rolvenden, and the school was now one member of staff less – relatively painlessly – and just when it needed to be.

A trip to Dungeness Lighthouse with Mrs Elliott and Miss Brown.

Of course, throughout all this background activity life carried on for the schoolchildren. Cookery and gardening classes at the Church Room had been abandoned – in their place came lessons at the Domestic Studies centre in Tenterden, to which the senior pupils travelled by bus once a week. The entirety of the playground was given over to tarmac where previously it had been half grass, organised games began on the Recreation Field, and recorders were introduced for music lessons. There were organised visits to the Romney, Hythe and Dymchurch Railway, Dungeness, Chessington Zoo (as it then was), farms to see sheep-shearing, a local bakery, and The Bridge Pottery on the Benenden Road. At the height of the debate as to staffing, the most memorable event to most pupils was the arrival of the fire brigade in December 1949, to attend to a panel of dado in the infants' room that had caught alight through proximity to the stove. This anthracite stove was a menace – when it wasn't threatening to burn the place down, it smoked incessantly when the wind was in the wrong direction.

Like her friend Mrs Edmonds before her, Mrs Elliott resigned in March 1951 to have her first child. In her place stepped another litany of short-term teachers: Mrs Butcher, Miss Waldron, Mrs Holden, Miss Isemonger, Mrs Tebbut. It was clear that some continuity was needed, and fortunately Miss Newman's health was robust enough to come back on to the staff from April 1953, by which time Mrs Elliott had returned. In addition, the predicted baby boom had become evident, and the school roll rose back to 130. This led to the appointment of another teacher, Sonia Butler, who joined in September 1953. There was some adverse comment about the increase in staff as ordered by the Education Committee – given the prolonged and unsettling debate about cutting staff only a few years earlier. But such doubts were dispelled by Miss Butler, who proved a success. Two years later she married and became Mrs Gardner, which is how most pupils now remember her.

The summer of 1953 saw the coronation of a new queen – the first such occasion any of the pupils had witnessed. As part of the celebrations a Coronation Beaker was presented to each child, and every class of the school gave a performance at the village festivities. A few weeks later they enjoyed a whole school trip to London to see the city festooned in flags and decorations. A feat that the newspapers were delighted to link with the coronation was also marked when a large party travelled to Tenterden to see *The Conquest of Everest* at the Embassy cinema. And there were further opportunities to learn about the Commonwealth when a Nigerian student of the University of London visited the school for four days in May 1954. His findings contributed to a report on the Weald of Kent by several foreign students, and subsequent years saw visitors from Bermuda and Rhodesia.

There was always the perennial issue of the school fabric. Some remedial work to the building was done in 1954 but this was really only papering over the cracks. The Kent Education Committee favoured replacing the school with a new one but, while similar discussions were happening with most other schools in the country – Wittersham and Tenterden being the closest examples – nothing was likely to happen quickly, and the staff and pupils continued to work in cramped, substandard conditions. But these were nothing compared to those of School House, which was considered to be almost uninhabitable on health grounds. The Education Committee were willing to allow its demolition, but would not pay for its replacement. Consequently, as with so much at Rolvenden, nothing was done about it.

Another important consideration was that local competition was opening up. Miss Clegg's little school at St David's had ceased, but there were now two local private schools: the Kingpost School at Merrington Place, and Mickledene School (later Ranters Oak) along the Benenden road. Rumours abounded that some parents who otherwise would have been happy to send their children to the primary school now favoured the private options simply due to the less cramped and more modern facilities on offer. There was friendly rivalry, but also co-operation: the 'Kingpost boys' are known to have used the school as a test centre for external examinations, taking them alongside the primary school pupils.

Eventually some compromises were reached with regard to the overcrowding at the school. A staffroom was provided by the conversion of one half of the air-raid shelter, with the other half given over to storage. In the absence of a school hall, the Church Room was used for drama, music and physical education. While a welcome solution, it was not an easy one – the managers were not satisfied with the general disrepair of the room and hygiene issues from the kitchen and lavatories. But in admitting that the schoolchildren were the heaviest users of the room, the school was compelled to contribute to the cost of putting things right. In addition, the increase in its use caused Mr Willcocks to worry more about the safety of children crossing the road outside the school. This issue was nothing new – a pupil had been hit and injured by a motorcycle as early as 1935 – but the mid-1950s saw a huge increase in the number of vehicles, and the roads were busier than ever. Lectures on road safety were a regular feature, but when plans were made to employ a crossing patrol at the corner, the police – incredibly – advised that it was not necessary. The staff were banned from taking the role by the teaching unions, who were worried about liability. Instead, what should have been an adult's job was done unofficially by two of the older children.

In May 1955, again in common with similar practice at other schools, a uniform was introduced. This is where Rolvenden School's distinctive and enduring colour scheme of yellow on brown stems from: brown blazers and yellow badges. It was understood at the time that Mrs Willcocks had chosen the colours herself, but it is worth noting that they bore a definite similarity to Mr Willcocks' own uniform from the Judd School in the 1910s. At around the same time the sporting pupils gained their own kit, as a precursor to being entered into the Weald of Kent School Sports Association competitions. Rolvenden's football and netball teams regularly played matches against other schools and performed creditably. But the competition was most fierce for the annual athletics tournament, hosted by different schools in rotation each June. The school entered a team for the first time at Headcorn in 1956 and, while they rarely won the silverware, it was always an enjoyable diversion.

Later that year the combined forces of Israel, Britain and France invaded Egypt, causing the Suez Crisis which led to widespread fuel shortages. To help ease the pressure on supplies, schools – including Rolvenden – opened in January 1957 a week later than usual, and the children enjoyed an extra-long Christmas holiday. In another sign of the times the managers recommended to the Education Committee that, thanks to the increasing use of machines, hop-picking no longer needed to be taken into account when setting the dates of the summer holiday. Over the next few years, the start date of the autumn term began to roll back from late to early September, in line with its position today. Also up for discussion was the see-saw nature of the school roll, which was now on a downward trend after the baby boom. One member of staff would have to be let go again. Miss Newman solved the issue by retiring through infirmity after some months of absence, during which her work was covered by Mrs Edmonds and Miss Groves. So ended a connection with Rolvenden School lasting over 30 years. Miss Newman remained an occasional visitor, with many friends in the village, until increasingly poor health caused her to lose her sight. She moved into a home for the blind in Ramsgate, where she died in 1983, aged 90.

ROLVENDEN
SPORTS
1960

Mrs Gardner left at the end of 1957, and her place was taken in the infants class by 43-year-old Marie Williams from Singleton near Ashford, who joined at the start of the following year. Mrs Elliott or Mrs Edmonds returned to help out on certain afternoons, and Miss Brown remained in the middle class, with Mr Willcocks taking the eldest pupils as usual. The school roll sank lower and lower, reaching under 70 pupils in 1959, in which year only two new pupils were admitted in September. The upside was that a whole classroom now lay empty, and for the first time the possibility was explored of moving the infants into it, and using the infants' school as a hall and canteen. The Kent Education Committee would only allow this if there was absolutely no possibility of it being needed for teaching again – as this assurance could not be given, the plan was shelved. This was particularly galling because Mr Willcocks and the managers were still unsatisfied with the state of the Church Room, and the headmaster continued to worry about the safety of crossing the road. But as a compromise the Committee paid for suspended ceilings to be fitted to the classrooms, starting with the oldest ones facing the road. Rather cynically, this was done to reduce the visible area of the rooms that needed redecoration, but once fitted they made an immediate difference in keeping the rooms warmer.

Shortly afterwards Mr Willcocks was compelled to spend a month in hospital, and the school was placed in the charge of Neville Clarke from Tenterden, a genial man who would later go on to serve as headteacher at Wittersham for 20 years. On Mr Willcocks' return he indicated that he would retire at the end of 1962, which gave the managers the opportunity to finally resolve the question of School House. Officially it had been condemned as uninhabitable, but while Mr Willcocks had professed himself quite comfortable there with his family, his replacement as headteacher might not be so content. Some were in favour of demolishing it. Others thought that if it could be brought up to a good state of repair, it should be done. Just a few months before Mr Willcocks' retirement the issue was settled by Historic England, who declared it to be of sufficient interest and merit to be a Grade II listed building which, thanks to the subsequent investment in remedial work, it remains.

Retirement gifts for Headmaster

Mr and Mrs Willcocks retired in December 1962 after 30 years at Rolvenden.

GIFTS FROM THE CHILDREN of Rolvenden C.E. Primary School were presented to the retiring headmaster, Mr. Willcocks, and Mrs. Willcocks, at the end of the school Christmas party.

Mr and Mrs Willcocks served Rolvenden School diligently and faithfully for exactly 30 years, guiding it through reorganisation, war, crisis and intense social change with a firm but kindly hand. The couple settled in Tenterden, and Mrs Willcocks died in 1979, aged 81. Her husband continued his outside interests in the arts, being a stalwart of the Tenterden Operatic and Dramatic Society and Tenterden Choral Society. He painted a portrait of Mayor Reuben Collison that now hangs in Tenterden Museum. Mr Willcocks always maintained a keen interest in his old school, and occasionally visited to recount stories from his time there to the pupils of the 1980s. His good friend Rev. John Green recounted that he was 'always interested, always busy… a most stimulating example to all OAPs, and indeed the young.' He died in 1992, aged 91.

Mr Willcocks' portrait of Reuben Collison, mayor of Tenterden.

Chapter 8

SPELLING IT OUT

1963-82

THE NEW HEADTEACHER, **John Howlett**, was born in St Helens, Lancashire, though moved with his family to London at the age of ten. He began teacher training in 1943, but was called up for military service before his career could begin. After three years in Germany as a paratrooper, he took his first teaching job in Huyton, Liverpool, where he met Phyllis Lowman, whom he married in 1950. Next came jobs at three schools in Bristol, and the arrival of sons Michael and Neville, before being appointed to Rolvenden – his first headship – from January 1963.

Mr Howlett lost no time in making his mark on Rolvenden. A Parent-Teacher Association was formed and began to host regular successful garden fetes and jumble sales. All teaching staff were encouraged to attend a handwriting course by the Italic Society of which Mr Howlett was a keen proponent. He introduced the competitive house system and gave them the names of medical scientists – Lister, Pasteur and Fleming – that remain to this day. As a focal event for the new houses, a School Sports competition day was first held in July 1963, with Harry Millum – ex-pupil and now chairman of the Layne Playing Field committee – generously offering the use of the field, ensuring that it was mown in readiness, and providing the winners' trophy. The event (won by Lister) was a great success and in future years alternated between the Layne field and Streyte recreation ground, with Mr Millum presenting the trophy in either case. This heralded a period of some success for the sporting pupils, with the athletics team winning the Percentile Cup at the Weald of Kent School Sports' Association tournament for the first time, and the football, netball and cricket teams enjoying similar victories at home and away fixtures.

A series of barriers to the advances that the authorities had closed off for years were suddenly lifted. A Road Crossing Patrol was approved by the police, and Walter Fagg was appointed to provide it. The Divisional Executive gave the go-ahead for central heating at last, which was installed over the first summer and proved very efficient, to everyone's delight. This coincided with the rearrangement of the school, so that all three classes were now in the main building adjacent to the road, and the old infants' room became the school hall for a short time. Mrs Howlett took her husband's class for two afternoons a week, allowing him to catch up with administrative duties, and for the first time a part-time secretary – Harry's wife Nina Millum – was formally employed. The pupils also enjoyed more frequent education trips – examples in Mr Howlett's first two years were to Rye and Camber, Headcorn Dairy, Canterbury, and the Kent Agricultural Show, with an additional trip for some to see the schoolboys' football between England and Germany at Wembley.

Mr Howlett with the football team.

There were, however, distinct challenges for the new headmaster. During his first winter at Rolvenden the school went without working lavatories for nine weeks, thanks to frozen and burst pipes. Then in March a chimney fire at the front of the school damaged the flue, pot and cowl, requiring extensive repair but providing much entertainment for the children. More sadly, the much-loved cleaner Ellen Irons suffered a stroke and died suddenly in July. The school was represented at her funeral by Mr Howlett and four pupils, and the managers noted that her death was 'a great loss to the school.' Her place was taken by Mrs Pellatt, and later Bill Monk and Norma Booker took over as joint cleaners. Mrs Williams left the infants' class in July 1964 and was replaced by Miss Somerville of Hastings, a dynamic teacher specialising in music. The large number of infants required the class to be split in two in the mornings, with Mrs Elliott teaching one half in the school hall, now returned to a classroom again.

Perhaps the defining achievement of Mr Howlett's headship, remembered by all pupils of the time, was the provision of a swimming pool. His idea was first presented to the PTA in October 1964. Within days the junior pupils had started doing odd jobs to help, and nearly £30 was raised this way by the end of the month. Money poured in from events such as jumble sales (£52), a teenagers' dance (£13), and collections of loose change at village football matches (£5), which was matched by the Rolvenden Men's Club. The fund was further strengthened by extraordinarily generous donations from David Barham (£50), Rolvenden Parish Council (£50), Kent County Council (£45) and a gentlemen named Alf Holyer, a one-time resident of the village from some 50 years previously, who sent a cheque for £20 after reading about the project in the *Kentish Express*. In all, the target of £525 was reached in just six months – an incredibly short space of time, especially compared to that of Wittersham, who took four years to raise the money for their school pool.

It was initially agreed to site the pool on the playground next to the hall, but this was changed to the front garden of School House. It was feared that its proximity to the road would cause problems, but Kent County Council gave their permission and the pool – an above-ground 'Mermaid' design from Sussex Pools Ltd – was erected in time for its official opening on 23rd July 1965. Mr Howlett gave a speech to over 100 parents present, and the ribbon was cut by seven-year-old prize winner Nicola Bridgeland. The new pool was an immediate and lasting success, used by pupils and villagers over the summer holidays, and supervised by the Howletts, Mrs Elliott or Miss Brown, all of whom had undertaken a special training course.

The newly-built swimming pool, in use from 1965.

Scenes from the 1965 Christmas production at the Church Room.

While the pool was built, a wider discussion was taking place regarding the purchase of land to be used as the school's own playing field. The field to the rear of the school was the obvious choice for many, but not Kent County Council, who preferred a piece of glebe land behind the Church Room – what is now Gybbons Road and Sumner Close. Their reasoning was that this would be the obvious place to re-site the whole school once the current buildings were no longer fit for purpose, and it was recommended that the land be bought under an 'educational reservation' for the future. It is unclear whether this was done, but this point in its history is the closest Rolvenden School came to being sold off and rebuilt elsewhere.

In the midst of this uncertainty, Mr Howlett was invited to become headmaster of the brand new Springdale Primary School in Poole, Dorset. He accepted and resigned his post at Rolvenden, leaving at the end of March 1966. He and Mrs Howlett were the subject of a special presentation at the Bull Inn, and showered with gifts and thanks. Their many services to the school were well out of proportion to the relatively short time they spent in Rolvenden. John Howlett spent five years at Springdale and then moved on to Broadstone Middle School, and in both schools his wife Phyllis also taught alongside him. After retirement in 1985 they settled in Broadstone where Phyllis died in 1997, aged 78, and John in 2013, aged 86.

Reg Spelling was born in Leighton in 1925 and joined the Royal Navy for the last years of the Second World War, serving in India, Sri Lanka and Burma. He undertook teacher training at Goldsmith's College, married Doreen Evans, and the couple both worked in a children's home at Chipping Norton before being posted to a British Forces school in Aden, Yemen, in 1958. When the Radfan Uprising threatened the country's stability and a state of emergency was declared, the family – with children Tim, Joanna and Simon – returned to the UK in 1964 and settled near Maidstone where Mr Spelling acted as a supply teacher, being sent all over Kent. He was appointed as Rolvenden's headteacher and began his post in April 1966, with Mrs Spelling quickly co-opted on to the staff to share Mrs Elliott's duties, taking her infants' class in the afternoons. The two couples quickly became firm friends.

There were further technological innovations too: in June the school and house were wired to the telephone network for the first time, and a few months later a class was taken over to School House to sit cross-legged on the floor and watch the BBC's *Merry-Go-Round* programme. As ever, where money was lacking it was made up for with invention: Mr Spelling and Ken Elliott recycled some old floorboards from Class 2 and fashioned them into a set of shelves.

Among the progress were difficulties and challenges: Mr Spelling and his staff had to deal with the tragic death of ex-pupil Andrew Iglinski, who had left the school only a week previously, in a swimming accident while on holiday. In respect, swimming at Rolvenden was cancelled, the headteacher and several pupils represented the school at his funeral and a sports cup – still presented today – was dedicated in his honour. Sad goodbyes and two presentation clocks were given on the retirements of Mrs Jenner, who had worked in the canteen since its establishment during the war, and caretaker Mr Fagg. The latter event took place during 1966's Harvest Festival celebration in the school hall, attended by over 60 parents and special guests Miss Newman and Miss Close, then aged 87. The hall was packed to overflowing, with 'no room for a cat' in Mr Spelling's words, though a pressman did manage to squeeze in and take a delightful photograph.

Walter Fagg's retirement presentation, September 1966.

In order to give the pupils the widest possible appreciation of the world, it was frequently arranged for visiting lecturers to deliver talks on various topics. Sometimes well-travelled locals came to talk – chief among these was Beatrice Lumley, mother of actress Joanna, bringing artefacts from Malaya and India which were 'a great success with the children.' Mr Spelling, too, could speak with authority on his many travels while in the Navy and in Aden. At other times, delegates from the Commonwealth Institute introduced such topics as The Maori People, A Visit to Australia, a Safari into Kenya and Canada Today, all illustrated with a filmstrip projector. Empire Day had by now become Commonwealth Day and was not celebrated as before, but Rolvenden's children had a good grounding in the wider world from the earliest possible ages.

Rolvenden's team and supporters at a Weald of Kent Schools Sports Association tournament.

The Commonwealth Institute delegates usually visited Wittersham School on the same day, and closer links were forged with the neighbouring school in a shared annual summer holiday for one week at St Mary's Bay. Other shared outings were to Chessington Zoo and to the Royal Tournament at Earl's Court – an exhausting day out in 1968 lasting nearly twelve hours. Miss Somerville left that year for a post in Brede, teaching music throughout the school there, and was replaced in September by Wendy Freeman, a caring and experienced teacher living at Hawkhurst, who took over the upper infants. Her appointment began a stable staff roster that lasted for a decade: Mr Spelling in Class 1; Miss Brown (for the time being) in Class 2; Miss Freeman in Class 3; and the infants of Class 4 shared by Mrs Elliott (in the mornings) and Mrs Spelling (in the afternoons).

Some of the most eagerly-awaited and fondly-remembered events of Mr Spelling's time were the Christmas festivities, which by the end of the sixties had settled into a regular format. A Christmas tree, generously provided by Hole Park, was set up in early December and decorated by the youngest children. The next two weeks were a blizzard of preparations and rehearsals for a community performance in the Church Room, initially a pantomime (*Aladdin*, *Cinderella*, *Humpty Dumpty*) but later replaced with a festive variety concert. A few days before the end of term was a Christmas party back at the Church Room with food and games, and for the first few years, the children were invited to perform their own 'turn' at the microphone. The quality of these were sometimes variable, so PTA funds were later used to buy a 16mm projector and the children enjoyed a film show instead. Then on the last day of term, everyone gathered for carols around the tree. This was a truly magical and memorable event, sometimes made more so by circumstance – in the industrial turmoil of the time, power cuts more than once caused the event to be held by candlelight.

The 1967 Christmas production of Aladdin, *and subsequent party.*

Sports Day, 1969.

When, in December 1969, an unprecedented teaching strike was called for, Mr Spelling – naturally conservative in outlook – pointedly resigned from the National Union of Teachers in disgust. There were already challenges enough: nothing further would be allowed to disrupt the education of Rolvenden's children if it could be avoided. Mr Spelling was further encouraged by the appointment as Education Secretary in June 1970 of one Margaret Thatcher, who announced a plan to modernise all Victorian primary schools, and whose future Navy Minister and resident of Rolvenden, Keith Speed, would later be elected to the Ashford constituency in 1974. Mr Spelling regarded Tenterden's (relatively) new purpose-built junior school with some envy, and was increasingly aware that the facilities there were more attractive, to some parents, than at Rolvenden. For those to whom the private sector was an option, there was the competitive edge enjoyed by nearby Ranters Oak School, in operation until the mid-eighties. Yet Mr Spelling always retained an appreciation for the unique heritage he was tasked to look after. At around this time, the centenary of the 1870 Education Act, he began to look into the history of the school, collecting photographs and interviewing members of the Parker and Oxley families. The results were collated into a successful exhibition, and sparked his enthusiasm for the local history of the area.

Class 4 (Mrs Elliott),
1971.

Class 3 (Miss Freeman),
1971.

Class 2 (Miss Brown),
1971.

Class 1 (Mr Spelling),
1971.

More innovations came the same year with the installation of a television in the school for the first time — something Mr Spelling had pushed for since his arrival — and the establishment of a film club, open to local children of any school, in which were shown educational films from the council, cartoons, and a *Just William* serial. It had to adapt to the challenges of the times — the delivery of the films was often disrupted by postal strikes, and as more families obtained televisions at home it lost its appeal — but was a bright success for a good few years.

Less satisfactory were the conditions in which the staff and pupils still had to work; an issue that never seemed to go away. In 1972 the HMI inspector again stated that the school needed urgent attention, either in modernising or replacing altogether. Mr Spelling was pleased that the surveyors they sent to assess the situation turned up in foul December weather:

> *What a day! Pouring rain, cold wind and school was seen in worst conditions, with puddles, blocked gutters etc. etc... They left in the knowledge that conditions here are far from ideal and on a bitterly cold, wet day they are most unpleasant.*

One surveyor was heard to remark: 'I wouldn't like to read *The Times* in these toilets.' Nonetheless, over the Christmas holidays an attempt was made to repaint them. By January much of this new paint had flaked off the walls with the damp.

Compounding the problem was the fact that the school was being used as a village facility, with the Women's Institute, Brownies and others making use of the buildings. Similarly, the annual Sports Day was by now a whole-village fixture, attracting large crowds and much enthusiasm. Seeing the opportunity for fundraising, refreshment stalls and raffles began. One year an enormous cake, iced in the school's colours of brown and yellow, was raffled and won by Mr Spelling amid many good-natured cries that the result was fixed. In 1973 table tennis was offered as a sport, leading to a team

May Day music, mid-1970s.

being entered at a Gillingham tournament, and with the demise of the film club a chess club was also started, with hockey in the Church Room being introduced later on.

However, it must be said that success still tended to elude Rolvenden in the inter-schools championships, to which Mr Spelling always transported the teams in his car, with occasional help from other parents. He was quick to remind his players that sportsmanship mattered above all, and was clearly frustrated when this was not observed by other teams. Sometimes Rolvenden came tantalisingly close, as in 1972 when the footballers were knocked out of the small schools' tournament by Biddenden (who, 'I found out afterwards, should have been in the large schools section') or in 1978 when a controversial handling offence from Woodchurch denied Rolvenden a place in the final. There was therefore justifiable pride in two football victories in a row from a strong team, in 1974-75.

Their success was no doubt boosted by the purchase of the playing field to the rear of the school. This process had taken a decade to resolve; being slowed by the reluctance of the authorities and complicated negotiations as to rights of way. Finally, in June 1974 Kent County Council completed the purchase. They warned that it could not be used by the pupils for some time, being uneven and pitted with holes which would take time and money to rectify. But feeling that they had waited long enough, the staff and pupils instead made a concerted effort to have it ready for Sports Day a month later, filling in the holes with earth every lunchtime until the surface was (relatively) flat and safe.

An aerial shot from 1973, showing the War Ag building and part of the new school field.

There remained the rusting eyesore that was the old War Ag building. Mr Spelling tried, without success, to find a scrap merchant willing to pull it down, take the materials away and clear the site. In October 1975 he asked the Hook family if they knew of anyone who might help, and then went on holiday to Wales over half-term. On his return in November he found that David and Michael Hook had started the job themselves ('this is really excellent'). By the New Year the building had disappeared, and Mr Spelling and the older pupils used the remaining breeze blocks to fashion a wicket for cricket practice. For this action the headmaster was reprimanded by the authorities ('I'm a bad lad... All my hard work and all the thanks I get is a telling-off') until, a few months later, the council's PE advisor inspected the work and agreed that it was safe to use. By then twenty oak trees had been planted on the site of the building and Mr Spelling noted with satisfaction that they would one day provide plenty of shade for the children 'but, alas, not in my lifetime.'

Doreen Moore of the PTA plants one of twenty new oak trees, March 1976.

These young trees were very nearly casualties of the infamously hot and dry summer that year, and were only saved by lines of pupils passing buckets across the playground to water them. There was little relief in swimming, as the water temperature regularly reached over 80 degrees Celsius, and in August the pool developed two leaks which put it out of use for the rest of the year. A plan to use Wittersham's pool foundered when theirs went out of service at exactly the same time. But the BBC brought some welcome excitement that same month when they cast several local children as extras in their serial *Katy*, an adaptation of Susan Coolidge's *What Katy Did* which was filmed at Biddenden, Benenden and Hawkhurst. Some were even required to visit the BBC studios in London and when the series was screened in October Mr Spelling commented that 'most of Rolvenden must have been watching... we enjoyed it very much.'

By now Mr and Mrs Spelling had established themselves as figures at the heart of village life; liked and greatly respected by many. There are multiple stories of those in Rolvenden who were bereaved, or suffering family crises, or were otherwise in need of help and found it at the Spellings' door. Hugs were readily dispensed by both. Mr Spelling was elected to both the parish council and the parochial church council, and was an active member of both. His wife, later described as 'the life and soul of social life,' was a loyal member of the WI and was particularly involved in the village's arts and crafts scene.

The Spellings maintained close friendships with all their colleagues, both past and present. When Miss Close died in 1974, aged 94, Mr Spelling led a delegation of staff to her cremation at Charing and later memorial service in Rolvenden. Miss Brown, who had been Miss Close's companion and carer for many years, was offered much support but took the opportunity to retire at the end of the year. She received a Parker pen, a dressing table and vanity set from the present pupils, and a further £62 contributed by many former pupils. This much-loved teacher of Rolvenden's children for nearly 30 years remained close to the village for the rest of her life, and died in 2010 at the grand age of 95. Her position at Rolvenden in 1975 was filled by Hilary Taylor, then 26 years old but with previous teaching experience at Blacklands and Malling. It was an inspired choice and Mrs Taylor would prove to be just as loved and enduring as her predecessor.

Miss Kathleen Brown, 1986.

These were times of high jinks and japes which have passed into Rolvenden legend: the time a recording of the Christmas concert was sent in to Ed Stewart at Radio 1 (he did not play it); or when Joanna Lumley visited the school and promised a tour of the LWT studios; or when the competing Ranters Oak display at the church flower festival was quietly dismantled overnight; or when the Silver Jubilee celebrations in 1977 were gamely continued through driving rain; or the stink-bomb in the piano (one of the very few times Mr Spelling was compelled to use corporal punishment); or the jolly to Ashford to see the Queen drive past on her way to the station. All stories, told with a smile, are testament to the sheer enjoyment of those years at the school as experienced by the pupils.

Trouble was brewing behind the scenes, however, over the staffing of the school as allowed by the Kent Education Committee. The school roll had dropped to a low of 73 pupils, meaning that a headteacher and four members of staff could no longer be supported. The Committee wanted it reduced to two full-time teachers and one part-time for just one-and-a-half days; Mr Spelling protested, and the part-time teaching was increased to four days. It required some uncomfortable remodelling with the infants from September 1976: Miss Freeman was required to take Class 3 in the mornings, then both Classes 3 and 4 in the afternoons. Nobody was happy with this arrangement – Mr Spelling said 'This economy depresses me beyond measure' – but he realised that there was no alternative. Despite all this, the staff remained outwardly cheerful and, to pupils and outsiders, the school was largely a very happy ship, something their headteacher was quick to appreciate:

> *It's good to have adaptable staff who work so conscientiously and happily – they are so dedicated and I am extremely lucky in so many ways.*

This was in spite of the state of the building, which was now critical. An indoor toilet had since been built for the infants, but with every small advancement there was a bigger setback. In November 1976 a mysterious fire destroyed a store at the end of the infants' room, and all equipment within was lost. Any improvement that was suggested by someone was held off by another, in the fear that it would jeopardise the hope held by many (including Mr Spelling) for a brand new school. In wet weather the trek to the Church Room for lunch was onerous and the toilets downright unpleasant, as the headmaster vented in anguish:

> *How much longer I wonder will it be necessary for us to have this irksome journey every dinner time? Oh for a hall of our own! Oh for a new school with indoor toilets!*

Whatever his private frustrations, Mr Spelling wasted no time in rolling up his sleeves to fix things when necessity arose. In November 1977 he returned home late from a function to find that the wind had lifted part of the PVC roof off the boys' toilets. Mrs Spelling found him trying to fix it back in to place in the pitch darkness, and was not impressed:

> *'What other headmasters would be up ladders and clambering on roofs at nearly one o'clock in the morning in the cold wind?' I could not answer!*

She had a point. Her husband was even less impressed by council surveyors who cancelled their visit to see the toilets due to bad weather – his pupils had no such option.

> *It's cold and miserable but the snow is light and continuous so the powers that be who want to improve the children's toilet facilities etc. will come another day.*

Worse was to come in 1978, which was a particularly torrid year for the school. Miss Freeman, who had been suffering health problems for some time, took extended leave at the start of the year – six weeks turned to three months, and then indefinitely. Mrs Spelling took on more duties but then was herself hospitalised for a double hip replacement – instead the roles were taken by Monica Scrowston of Goudhurst and Lynda Watts, just prior to her appointment to Wittersham. She remembers Mr Spelling constantly spraying disinfectant in an attempt to keep a circulating virus at bay (it was particularly bad that year), and filling up the classroom heaters with oil every afternoon. In April one of these heaters gave Class 3 a nasty surprise:

> *Suddenly we had a small bang from the stove... fumes from the top and a much louder bang resulted in the children huddling at the other side of the room in a frightened group... We put our coats on and 'invaded' Class 4 and Mrs Elliott looked after the two classes while I cautiously opened Class 3's door. The room was filled with smoke; the two lids had been blown off the burners and one burner was actually burning with flames coming out at the top... The room was filthy but once the oil had all been used up... the children were able to return.*

Two days later came the news that further staffing could no longer be avoided, and that from September the staff would be reduced to Mr Spelling, Mrs Taylor and Miss Freeman, with Mrs Spelling taking three half-days. Mrs Elliott, being the closest to retirement age, would be compelled to leave – which Mr Spelling regarded as 'a thought which I dread.' But by now Miss Freeman had been diagnosed with an advanced cancer, and it was clear that she would not be returning. The speed of her decline surprised everyone, and it was a great shock when Mr Spelling announced to the school in September that she had died at Hawkhurst Cottage Hospital.

> *Our deep sadness is tempered by time and knowledge that she was terribly ill and her case a hopeless one... A very emotional time for us all, but, as we emphasised to all the children, Wendy wanted them to know she loved them very much, so we went about our day's work with hope-filled hearts.*

One result of this sad event was that Mrs Elliott moved to full-time work in Miss Freeman's place – though as she was nearly due to retire, it could only be a temporary solution. Then to cap off this year, in December a motorcyclist came off his bike at Church Corner and ploughed into six infants as they were walking to lunch. The police arrived: statements were taken, and the children checked over by Dr Gompertz of Tenterden. Thankfully, there were no serious injuries.

The football team were runners-up at a Weald of Kent tournament, March 1978.

Class 3 (Mrs Elliott), 1979.

Class 2 (Mrs Taylor), 1979.

Class 1 (Mr and Mrs Spelling), 1979.

It took this incident as a catalyst for something to be done about the school accommodation. Walking back and forth across two busy roads for lunch would no longer be an option. Instead, the managers agreed that the old original schoolroom, then partitioned and occupied by Classes 1 and 2, would be converted into a multi-purpose hall with a servery. Class 1 would move into a smaller room then used for television viewing, and Class 2 into a mobile classroom purchased and erected on-site. It sounded neat on paper. In reality, it took eighteen months to achieve, with a shed to the rear being demolished, the partition taken down, the servery building delayed by rain ingress, and difficulties in finding an available mobile (rumour had it that an Ashford school didn't want to let it go). In the middle of all this work, the value of the project was confirmed when another lunchtime accident occurred at Church Corner. This time a trailer loaded with a digger, being pulled by a tractor, overturned, spilling oil everywhere and blocking the whole road for the rest of the day.

Nina Millum retired as secretary after 15 years' work and was replaced by Elaine Dixon. Then Mrs Clarke and Mrs Francis gave way to Janet Hoad and Avril Bryant as midday supervisor and kitchen assistant, with Dina Wood taking on the road crossing patrol duty. When Class 2 finally moved into their mobile in September 1980 Mrs Taylor was absent on maternity leave, returning in the New Year. By this time the reconstruction project was complete, with the new hall and servery opening in October 1980 and proving an immediate success. No more tramping to the Church Room and back every day in all weathers; lunches from now on would be drier, smarter and happier. And that year's Christmas party was held in the hall, all pupils together, for the very first time.

October 1980: lunches move from the Church Room (left) to the School Hall (right).

Mrs Elliott's retirement presentation, February 1982.

Mrs Elliott returned for a while in the spring of 1981 but it was clear that retirement was beckoning, and Maralyn Button – living in Rolvenden but latterly teaching at Sandhurst – was called in to take her place; initially for three mornings a week, then full-time from 1982: an arrangement that would last for over two decades. With her family outlook and community spirit, Mrs Button would prove to be yet another ideal appointment. Mrs Elliott was presented with her retirement gifts (a Kenwood mixer, and cassette storage case) in February 1982, ending an association with the school, as both pupil and teacher, that had lasted for nearly fifty years. She remained a much-loved figure in Rolvenden, with many friends, and died in 2008, aged 84.

The school roll rose a little in 1982, allowing an extra part-time member of staff to be taken on: this was Judy Parton, previously at Wittersham, and an ex-pupil of the school herself, being the daughter of Mrs Edmonds. At the same time as Mrs Elliott's retirement, Mr Spelling announced to the governors that he also wished to retire at Easter. It was something of a bombshell, requiring a scramble to appoint a headteacher for the first time in nearly 20 years. As this could not be done in time for Easter, Mrs Spelling took over in Class 1 while her husband remained in a non-teaching capacity for one further term, carrying on with administrative duties. When the time came in July for this most devoted couple to shake hands with their pupils for the last time, there was barely a dry eye in the school. Over a hundred people attended their farewell presentation (the ubiquitous Kenwood mixer, along with a sandwich toaster and cheque for £173). Like Mr Willcocks before him, Mr Spelling had wished to remain in School House but his offer to buy it was denied by red tape. Instead he and his wife moved to Tenterden where they again established themselves as pillars of the community. Mr Spelling pursed his interest in sports and local history, researching and writing several books, and Mrs Spelling continued as a doyen of the WI and was active in the town's Operatic and Dramatic Society. Reg Spelling died in 2001, aged 76, and Doreen in 2018, aged 94. They are extremely fondly remembered as a couple who loved the surroundings in which they lived and worked, and gave a good deal of themselves back to the people they served.

Chapter 9

END OF A CENTURY

1982-2000

BORN IN GILLINGHAM, the new headteacher **John Drywood** had trained at Bromsgrove with a BEd degree from the University of Birmingham, before gaining plenty of teaching experience back in Kent at both primary and secondary level. Locally, he worked at Woodchurch and St Michaels (as Deputy Head) before being appointed to Rolvenden in 1982.

Mr Drywood's time at Rolvenden did not start under the best of circumstances. When he took over that September, he found that Class 1 was missing its floor. The builders had removed the old floor at the start of the summer holidays but had then been delayed in fitting a new one. It was finally done on the Friday before term started, causing a mad all-weekend scramble – with the help of the Booker family – to get the classroom refurnished, restocked and ready for teaching. This chaos was indicative of the accommodation issues that had caused Mr Spelling such a headache, and which Mr Drywood largely inherited. He shared his predecessors' concerns about the proximity of the main road, the condition of the lavatories (again) and he compiled a long list of repairs which, he hoped, would be listened to.

John Drywood, headteacher from September 1982.

The concern most easily remedied was the lack of an office and storage space, which was a considerable handicap to running the school in a modern and efficient manner. The solution was to convert the remainder of the air-raid shelters into a shared office for the headteacher and secretary, a staffroom and a storeroom. No sooner had this been done — over the summer of 1983 – than a combination of wet rot, dry rot and woodworm caused the floor of Class 3 to collapse, requiring further repairs. Still the community willingly gave money where the council could not: a marvellous £500 was raised at that year's Summer Fayre for the renovation of the swimming pool.

Charity was also evident in the many good causes to which Rolvenden children gave at this time: the relief of Polish children in 1983 (living under martial law imposed by the communist government) for whom Mrs Lumley collected gifts, letters and decorated soaps to send; the 1984 Ethiopian famine appeal championed by Bob Geldof; the perennial Cancer Research fund; and later on, for victims of the Armenian earthquake and Clapham Junction rail disaster. With a view towards mutual understanding and dialogue, a link was established with the Julianaschool in Eibergen, Holland, and Class 1 kept up a regular correspondence by letter.

The school's first computer, a BBC-B, was installed in 1984.

The march of technology continued apace, with the widespread use of computers in schools beginning in the early 1980s. Chief among these was the BBC-B model, which was greatly coveted, but its price tag of £400

seemed well out of reach, especially in light of everything else that had been asked for. Rolvenden Men's Club promptly stepped up and offered to help, and over the course of a year raised £350 towards the machine, which was bought and installed in February 1984. At the same time Class 1 had the opportunity to make their own 30-minute television feature using a state-of-the-art home camera kit, for which Mrs Lumley gamely allowed herself to be interviewed. As part of the project they learned some of the craft of programme-making at the Kent Educational

Television Centre in Dover, while the younger classes visited the castle. The tape of their efforts remained at school to be viewed at leisure, if the timing worked out – the school now had a quarter-share in a new VHS video player that spent three of every four weeks at either Tenterden, St Michaels or High Halden schools. It was supplemented by a new television set, stand and shelf towards which Tenterden Lions Club had given £250.

As a keen musician it was inevitable that the performing arts would take on a new shine under Mr Drywood's leadership. Christmas performances continued with the familiar repertoire of nativity retellings – *Trig Trog and the Christmas Children*; *A Legend of Three Kings*; *Baboushka* – all of which were well attended and enthusiastically received. But the defining production of these years was 1984's *Smike*, a lavish musical based on part of Charles Dickens' *Nicholas Nickelby* which tied in nicely to a Class 1 English topic – they had previously visited Dickens-related sites in Rochester for the same purpose. Held over two nights in the school hall, it was produced in conjunction with the church choir and Homewood School, and featured visiting luminaries John and Margaret Roylance as Mr and Mrs Squeers, and a four-piece band led by the vicar, Rev. John Wright, shortly before he moved away to Cheriton.

The school's joinr production of Smike, *1984.*

Mr Drywood also shared his predecessor's particular interest in local history, and each year mounted a community-focused event at the school highlighting Rolvenden's heritage. March 1984 saw a 'Pictures of the Past' exhibition of over a hundred photographs and the following year saw the children curate a museum of 'How we used to live.' Class 1 undertook a history project on the ancient ship found near Maytham Wharf in 1822, and visited Hexden Channel and the moat at Lowden Farm. Rolvenden became such a model school in this regard that Mr Drywood was invited to deliver a talk to other teachers on 'Medieval Times in Primary School History.'

Changing village scene on display

Harry Millum points out an old picture of himself to Headmaster John Drywood and Rolvenden Primary School pupils Tina Back and Deborah Crane.

PICTURES of the past, an exhibition illustrating changes in the life of the village during this century, was opened at Rolvenden Primary School by the Mayor of Ashford, Cllr Jo Winstitrith.

The exhibition, the idea of Headmaster John Drywood, was organised with the help of David Millar, warden of Ashford Teacher's Centre. Items on display were donated by local residents.

Many visitors identified themselves

Harry Millum, chairman of the school's governors for the past 17 years, pointed out himself with his brother in 1924, and dancing with his daughter in the Fifties.

It is hoped that local people will add to this collection of Rolvenden memorabilia.

The photographs will be kept to be used by the children.

Mr Drywood said: "This is a way of bringing ... into the children's ...

Kentish Express March 21st. 1985

School's 'good old days'

PUPILS HAVE FUN MAKING A MUSEUM

...STERS at ...en primary ...ad a great time ...rning their ...hall into a ...

...collection of ...ating items ...from 1902 were ...ed together by ...pils, after their ...t was stimulated ...visit to Folkestone ...nes.

...result of their ...ork was a comprehensive display ...Queens How We ...to Live — An in... ...nto the past.

...e exhibition it ...e topics such as ... Life, Home, ...On the Farm, At ...and At Work.

...ls had written to ...

many museums and received assistance and in some cases loaned of exhibits. Sally Tomkins obtained information from Tunbridge Wells and received a lorgnette with patented spring dating back to 1825.

Karen Hall, in touch with London's Imperial War Museum, found details of a Next of Kin plaque supplied by Julie Mitchell of

Rolvenden Layne, bearing the name of Charles Sharpe, one of her relatives.

Jennifer Smith's ration book: a First World War gas mask; 1929 Singer Sewing Machine; 1938 copy of Radio Times.

There were so many pieces from the past to interest visitors, including many photographs, including one taken by the Kent Messenger of Rolvenden school's pupils in 1929.

Cleaner

Miss Mileson of Freezingham Cottages, Rolvenden, paid £38 for a vacuum cleaner in 1928 — and the machine ...

when he obtained a scholarship to Cranbrook school.

On display were three of his exercise books and visitors were able to see his neat drawings of animals, writing and geometry as he recalled the days when he created such tidy work.

Headmaster John Drywood said he was delighted with the response, especially from local residents.

Pupils dig in for Tree Week

YOUNGSTERS at Rolvenden county primary school have branched out from their classrooms to plant 90 trees alongside their playing field.

The planting was part of National Tree Week, and is part of a long-term conservation project at the school.

Growth

Some pupils have adopted trees planted earlier — and the fast-growing specimens are already outstripping their own rate of growth.

A nature garden and woodland area are being created and by the time the school celebrates its 150th anniversary next April the children are aiming to have completed a nature trail.

Kent County Council's property services department arranged for pupils from 16 schools to take part in the Tree Week planting of 3,200 saplings including oak, ash, beech, hornbeam, field maple, wild cherry, alder and willow.

Colin Barham tries out an ...

Plant

John Parker, principal landscape manager, said: "Planting trees is a wonderful way to interest children in the environment and landscape around them.

"It is very satisfying to

TENTERDEN and district Lions president Micheal Tredway (right) hands over a cheque to Rolvenden primary school headmaster Mr John Drywood last Friday. The money is to help the school buy its own television set.

Mr Drywood received the cheque on behalf of the PTA which also raised £250 towards the purchase, thus relieving the school of rental fees. Accompanying Mr Tredway was his wife Nicky, and Gordon Stonham, a Rolvenden Lions member. On hand to welcome them were members of the PTA and some of the school's pupils.

TAILOR MADE!

ROLVENDEN Primary School headmaster, Mr John Drywood, should not find his part too difficult when he treads the boards tonight (Friday), and tomorrow in a production of the musical Smike — his role is that of a headmaster.

He will not be Squeers, the cruel master in Dickens' Nicholas Nickleby on which the musical is based, but a present day headmaster who shocks his new school by replacing the usual English lesson with a production of the play, with the pupils taking part.

It is a joint venture between the

primary school, the church choir and Homewood School and is being directed by Mr Drywood in the school hall. Musical director is Rolvenden's vicar, the Rev John Wright, whose son William is playing Nickleby on the first night.

Another Homewood School pupil, Paul Gardener, plays the part tomorrow when a second cast takes on the children's role.

Smike is played by Joanna Woods and Katrina Light from the primary school, while sisters Hazel and Sonia Hemsley, of Homewood, are both Sammy Squeers. The part of Squeers goes to John Roylance, the newly-appointed headmaster of St Mark's Primary School in Tunbridge Wells. His wife, Margaret, a teacher at Tenterden, plays Mrs Squeers.

For all your DIY material under one roof

TREV'LL

Stepping out on £300 walk

ROLVENDEN Primary School playing field was the scene for a test of stamina for 34 youngsters taking part in a sponsored walk arranged by the school's parent teacher association.

The participants plodded on for five miles, completing 20 laps around the field. More than £300 was raised by the event which will be used for the swimming pool fund.

A plastic liner will cost £300 and another £300 is needed for general repairs to the pool.

A SPONSORED walk by more than 30 pupils of Rolvenden County Primary School on Saturday last week is expected to have raised more than £300 towards repairing the school's learner swimming pool and providing a liner for it. Organised by the parents association, the 20-lap walk — about five miles — was around the sports field. Headmaster Mr John Drywood is pictured with some of his pupils who took part in the sponsored walk.

On the same theme, in 1985 the BBC began the Domesday Project to mark 900 years since the original Domesday survey, and Rolvenden's pupils were enthusiastic contributors. They canvassed the village with questionnaires, conducted interviews and researched the local industries, facilities and clubs. Their findings are illuminating and reflect concerns and attitudes that still endure 35 years on:

> *Rolvenden is a super village. It has been said that a village without its own Vicar, School and Cricket Club loses its soul. We are fortunate in having all three, so that we have a 'soul.'*

> *We feel that not enough is done for youngsters of today. We can see the village growing older and older as prices of property go up and more and more retired people move into the village.*

> *While it is important that certain amenities should be provided it is vital that the rural charm and village atmosphere should be preserved. This is an exceptional village.*

Clearly, Rolvenden was regarded as a worthy and attractive place to live. This was mirrored in continued efforts to improve the school's own environment, with a nature trail, garden and pond laid and dug ready for the spring of 1986. The aim was to provide several types of nature habitat: marsh, meadow, shrubs, hedge, logs, rocks and stones. For National Tree Week over 170 native saplings – hornbeam, beech, ash, maple and oak – were planted on the school field. All these efforts helped to secure Rolvenden's win as the Best Kept Village in Kent, and were mentioned in the official citation. Later on, the school won a Heritage and Environment Award worth £100, which was spent on a polaroid camera and binoculars.

The lovely setting was not reflected in the state of the school buildings, which continued to be a major bugbear. In February 1986 – the coldest for 40 years – the outside toilets froze five times, and conditions helped illness to cut a swathe through the children and staff, laying low for several weeks both Mr Drywood (tracheitis) and Mrs Taylor (influenza). The Area Education Officer attended the PTA's Annual General Meeting later that year and was given a rough ride by angry parents demanding improvements. Finally, the council was compelled to intervene. Within weeks an architect had drawn up plans for the remodelling of the

Mr Drywood inspects the facilities.

school. A square atrium would be formed with the hall to its south-east and 1912 extension to its south-west. A new classroom would be built to its north-west, and for the first time, the main building would be linked with the infants' classroom, with offices for the headteacher and secretary, staffroom and extra toilet block filling the gap between them. The plans were exciting and invigorating and met with general approval; yet in 1986 it would all still be some way off.

By far the defining event of Mr Drywood's tenure was the extraordinary celebration of 150 years since the building of the school, which took place over several weeks in 1987. It was an opportunity to celebrate with the community, many of whom had attended the school and were delighted to lend their support. Pupils visited the church to see the parish records and notable graves, and Hole Park to learn about the school's link with the Gybbon family. A celebratory school magazine ran for three editions, and attractive commemorative plate was produced. That year's play, *Oliver Twist*, was exactly contemporaneous with the school, the story having been written in 1837.

Friday 1st May saw the celebrations kick off with a procession of garlands (made under the supervision of Mrs Parton) to the vicarage, the sheltered housing at Monypenny, and finally to Great Maytham. Harry Millum opened an exhibition of Victorian Rolvenden in the school hall, and Class 1 showed off the maypole dancing they been rehearsing for weeks. The following day, an informal reunion of old teachers, pupils and friends saw members of the Parker family mingle with Mr Willcocks, Mr Spelling and many other representatives of the school's past.

Then on Bank Holiday Monday, 4th May, came the crowning event of the PTA's May Day Fayre, which took on the Victorian theme. A gaggle of pupils made their way excitedly to Tenterden Town station, where they greeted the arrival of their guest of honour, Queen Victoria a.k.a. Norma Booker, gamely playing the part in full costume, and driven by Christopher Booth in a vintage car from Rolvenden Motor Museum. The party alighted at Wittersham Road and made their way to the school via the Layne; the regal visitor following in pony and trap. An afternoon of festivities was then enjoyed with a prize draw, rides, games, dances, and traditional Victorian diversions.

The successful 150th anniversary celebrations, 1987.

These memorable and successful celebrations were (almost) Mr Drywood's swansong. Weeks later, he was appointed headteacher of Sutton Valence Primary School, to begin in January 1988. His last months at Rolvenden were rather bumpy: a chicken-pox epidemic broke out; the Sports Day was postponed and then cancelled due to bad weather; the school was burgled and the television and video recorder stolen; and finally, in October, the Great Storm closed all Kent schools and left roads impassable and the village without power for four days. Mr Drywood spent eight years at Sutton Valence, four years at Woodchurch and then two years' teaching in Singapore. He and wife Linda now live in retirement in Gloucestershire.

Back to 1988, no permanent headteacher had been appointed for the first months of the year, so the school was placed in the hands of Miss Hewitt from the Kent supply pool. After eight years' service Mrs Dixon resigned as secretary, to be replaced by Sue Clout, and Andrew Butler – the new organist and choirmaster at the church – began as peripatetic music teacher, thus starting a connection to the school which would last for over three decades. His efforts were supplemented by those of Maralyn Button's mother Mrs Bowles, who accompanied many school performances. By April a new headteacher was also ready to join the staff – he was **Barry Dixon**, previously of Hastings. A very professional man with a keen sense of correctness and procedure, his apparent formality disguised a hidden streak of light-heartedness and fun which, when displayed, was greatly appreciated and remembered.

By now the long-awaited improvements to the school site had been formally approved, and not before time: Sue Clout recalls that, in their shared office, she had to stop typing whenever the headteacher took a telephone call so that he could hear what was being said. But there would be more disruption before the extension was ready for use: work was scheduled to begin in July and last until the following March. The start of the building coincided with the joint retirement of three of the school's longest-serving and most dedicated governors: Harry Millum, Eric Tiltman and Beatrice Lumley – who between them had done much to get the project off the ground.

For nine months, then, the staff and pupils picked their way around piles of bricks, sand and rubble, and did their best to block out the constant noise. The work was finished on time, and the staff spent their Easter holiday organising the move and stocking the new classrooms. An official opening on 29th April was marked by the sounding of bells from the church opposite. Despite his retirement as governor, Harry Millum was brought back as the guest of honour, and dutifully unveiled the plaque in the company of VIPs, parents and children. Then for a photograph, the pupils held a ribbon around the school which was later cut into pieces and presented to them with a commemorative certificate. Country dancing and games followed, and the cutting of a huge celebratory cake made by Mrs Clout. Mr Dixon later reported that news of the school's facilities had spread, and he was having to deal with plenty of enquiries from far-off parents who now wished their children to come to Rolvenden.

The Governors of Rolvenden County Primary School wish to invite

_____

to attend the Opening Ceremony of
The New School Extension
on Saturday 29th April 1989 commencing at 2.30 p.m.
Please assemble in the School Hall

R.S.V.P.
The Head Teacher
at the School

£157,000 school
extension opens

THE OUTSIDE toilets and offices in an old air raid shelter have become just a memory at Rolvenden Primary School which saw the unveiling of a new £157,000 extension on Saturday.

More than 200 adults and children celebrated the occasion and former pupil Mr Harry Millum, a former chairman of the governors for 22 years, unveiled a commemorative plaque.

Among the guests were Mrs Brenda Trench, chairman of the Kent Education Committee, Ashford MP Mr Keith Speed who lives in the village, and former pupils and staff.

Children entertained the guests with songs, poetry readings, music and maypole dancing. A ribbon was strung around the entire school, which is now under one roof. Each child is to be presented with a special certificate to mark the occasion by which will be attached a piece of the ribbon.

School secretary Mrs Sue Clout baked a commemorative cake and the headmaster Mr Barry Dixon said it had been a wonderful day for the school.

The new extension is opened, April 1989.

Despite the improvements, there were always unforeseen challenges to overcome. The crime spree that had begun in the autumn of 1987 continued: an attempted break-in was discovered in February 1988 (nothing was taken, though a window was removed and others damaged) and in December 1989 intruders set off the burglar alarm, which frightened them away. A month later, the Burns' Day Storm caused the pupils to be sent home at lunchtime when the school lost all heat and light. This proved to be a wise decision: hours later, when the building was empty of children, a chimney stack collapsed and fell through the servery roof, causing considerable damage.

Barry Dixon memorably joined in with the production of Aladdin, *December 1989.*

Nonetheless there were still continued excitements and excursions. May 1989 saw the school's first residential trip, to Seaford, accompanied by Mr Dixon and Mrs Parton – it proved so successful that a more ambitious trip to France was undertaken the following year with pupils from Salehurst. Mr Dixon gave a spirited and memorable performance as Widow Twangey in the school's production of *Aladdin* at Christmas 1989, despite an outbreak of flu having reduced the number of intended participants by over half.

The school in 1989.

The following spring, the pupils were taken to see parachutists landing in a field behind the Bull Inn to celebrate the opening of a restaurant. The school's summer fete hosted a group of Viking re-enactors who staged a battle and set up 'living history' tableaux. And while the school's own pool remained in use, a whole-school swimming treat was arranged at Tenterden's brand new leisure centre in April 1990. They returned six months later to see the building officially opened by the Princess of Wales and, thanks to a broken pump, continued to use the newer facility until a replacement could be found and fitted.

Great changes were now afoot in education; mostly a consequence of the introduction of a new National Curriculum. Computing was regarded as of vital importance and Mrs Parton became involved with the selection of Rolvenden as part of a countywide working party on the assessment of information technology. A second computer arrived: an RM Nimbus model, and one installed in the school office for the first time. The school said goodbye its dedicated remedial teacher Mrs Edmonds, and kitchen assistants Mrs Bryant, Mrs Bashford and Mrs Moore, and welcomed in their places Mrs Chappell, Mrs Tiltman and Mrs Brady. Mrs Ramsden joined as a part-time Class 1 teacher, freeing up Mr Dixon for administrative tasks. Classroom assistants were also introduced, with Jane Doyle one of the first in this role from January 1992. Mrs Doyle would quickly become an active participant in the PTA, serving on the committee for many years.

It was during Mr Dixon's time that the school embraced May Day celebrations which became a key feature of the year. Mrs Parton – now Mrs Burvill – who had taken on the responsibility of the garlanding and maypole dancing for the 1987 celebrations, continued with the same role for each subsequent year. To help encourage the sun on the appointed day, she wore a yellow jacket – a lucky talisman that worked every year except one. The yearly event was well-supported by parents and the children loved it; every photograph sparkles with glee.

After four years Mr Dixon was appointed headteacher at Harcourt County Primary in Folkestone, and left in July 1992 with many good wishes and 'many happy memories' of his time at Rolvenden. His successor was **John Rivers**, then acting headteacher at Boughton near Canterbury. Originally from Bexley, Mr Rivers had extensive experience both in Bexleyheath and for seven years at a school in Germany, but Rolvenden was his first substantive headship.

May Day celebrations during the 1990s.

He found a staff who were 'very supportive and friendly' and a school which very much played to his strengths as a community-minded person. In his first week he was visited by Rev. Anthea Williams, then parish deacon before becoming a vicar, who discussed greater integration with the church and agreed to deliver an assembly and attend lunch at the school each week. The Gybbons Trust made a donation of £100 to the school. Rolvenden Football Club had recently begun sessions for the pupils, and agreed to replace, erect and paint a new goal on the school field to replace the old, rotten one. 'What wonderful support we have!' the new headteacher commented. 'Without [it], like all the parents' support we are lucky to call upon from time to time, our village school would just not get the facelifts it deserves.'

It also worked the other way: the school field was regularly made available for village events, and a new photocopier was obtained that was better-able to handle the many requests for its use from community organisations. A tradition was also started whereby the children distributed Harvest offerings around the village. And the school community threw itself into Rolvenden's efforts for the Best Kept Village competition in 1993, prettifying the front adjacent to the road with new trees, plants and a flower border.

The school in 1994.

When Mr Rivers arrived the school was experiencing one its periodic dips in pupil numbers, which were languishing in the mid-fifties. The consequence was that money, allocated per pupil by the education authority, was not as forthcoming. Nonetheless he took steps to bring the teaching resources up to date, replacing the 1970s-era textbooks with the new Ginn Mathematics and Oxford Reading Tree schemes that had just been introduced. But modern teaching and the advent of the National Curriculum, as he also identified, put much more pressure on a school's finances. Classes in art, music and physical education were now formalised and needed to be funded, and it was recognised that the PTA played an important role in that respect. In these years they were able to provide money for vital resources and equipment through such events as coffee mornings, discos, bazaars, fetes and – a particular highlight of Rolvenden's social year – an annual Barbecue and Barn Dance evening.

The most pressing concern, as far as money went, was over the school's pool which by now had 'succumbed after years of use by energetic children.' Replacing it was a difficult 'sell' to some people, who pointed to the facilities at Tenterden which were much enjoyed as an alternative. But it was recognised that the advantages to Rolvenden's pupils, and indeed the wider community, would be greater, with its use open to all villagers and the Mother and Baby group. The scheme was kicked off by a donation from the newly-established Basil Russell Trust, set up as a legacy for the benefit of Rolvenden's young people. Once this money was secured, the floodgates opened, with champion fundraisers being the landlords of the Bull Inn, Mike and Brenda McDonough, who gathered over £1000 during 1994 with two Fun Days and a bottle for loose change on the bar. An enduring fundraising event was an annual Grand Fireworks Display which ran for several years, raised thousands, and is fondly remembered. Drawing on the goodwill of local builders, the pool was rebuilt and opened in 1995, with governor Kim Booker acting as its dedicated caretaker and technician for several years. As before, it opened over the summer holidays for all to enjoy the new facility.

Pub fun pools in cash

THE Bull at Rolvenden has raised more than £1,000 towards the new swimming pool for the village primary school.

Mike and Brenda McDonough presented the cheque on Tuesday after holding fun days with obstacle courses and barbecues in the pub garden.

The whole village has supported fund-raising events and the school is more than half way towards its £6,000 target.

It is hoped that a pool can be sunk next April.

More than 500 joined the school to raise the same amount of pounds for the pool fund on Fire-work Night.

The bonfire was lit by Oliver Sayer, Robert Taylor and James Taylor, who designed the best posters to advertise the event.

MAKING A FINE SPLASH AT ROLVENDEN

BRENDA and Mike McDonough cut the ribbon while Rachel Booker and Francesca Haywood are poised to take the first swim in the new swimming pool at Rolvenden School on Monday.

Mike and Brenda represented The Bull public house where £1,500 was raised for the new pool. Kent Education Authority, the school's PTA and the Basil Russell Trust also contributed.

To mark the fiftieth anniversary of VE-Day in May that year, which tied in with a designated 'Europe Day', an amateur radio station was set up (callsign GB0EUR) for the school's pupils to communicate with France. Having worked with computers since the mid-1970s, Mr Rivers also pushed for the school's technology to be updated. This coincided with the early days of email, and correspondence via CompuServe was set up between Rolvenden and a schools all over the world, such as Mr Rivers' old school in Germany and one in Ohio. That same year, Anita Bond, originally from Cheshire, joined from Staplehurst School as a part-time teacher and SENCO, with the duty of co-ordinating the provision for those with special educational needs.

Thanks to a great deal of community support, a new pool opened in 1995.

John Rivers left a school at which pupil numbers had almost doubled and was now in a sound financial position with no threat of closure. After Rolvenden he spent four years as headteacher of Headcorn Primary, then worked as a senior teacher at two Folkestone secondary schools. After some years active in the community of his home village of Wittersham, he is now retired in New Romney.

Barbara Scott at the White Cliffs Experience Roman Day, 1997.

Barbara Scott, who took over as headteacher from September 1996, was one of the first cohort of students to take the BEd degree at Merton College, Oxford. After some years in the Kent supply pool she held positions at Beaver Green and New Romney, where she became Deputy Head. Mrs Scott appreciated the school's 'very good ethos' which chimed with her own, and her time at Rolvenden was imbued with calm professionalism and a good deal of sound common sense. The sports teams were congratulated in success and consoled in defeat, but always reminded that good sportsmanship was paramount in either event – a lesson they rarely failed to acknowledge. The children were taught to appreciate the good things they enjoyed – 'particularly living in the garden of Kent' – while reflecting on those who had little. And as for the seasonal bunfight at the end of the year:

> *We do hope that none of us forgets the real meaning of Christmas. The staff do ensure that our children also have a time for quiet reflection and a chance to think about why Christmas means more than just presents and food.*

HMI had now been replaced by the Office of Standards in Education, or OFSTED, who undertook a national programme of inspections on a cycle of between four and six years. Rolvenden's turn came around in October 1997. Despite the inevitable stress caused by an unfamiliar three-day period of inspection, interview and examination, the school achieved a most pleasing result. It was regarded as a good school, with particular praise for the quality of its teaching, clear leadership, and attainments above the national average in English and science. Particularly praiseworthy comments were made on the caring and supportive nature of the school. As far as the new system of national standards went, Rolvenden had passed its first test.

The caring nature of the school was praised by OFSTED in 1997.

The work done previously to establish village relations was very much built upon, and Mrs Scott was delighted by the support received by the school from the wider community. Hundreds of Tesco and Sainsburys vouchers for computer equipment poured in from shoppers, funding a new Apple eMate 300 portable computer, and a similar Co-op scheme paid for a frame to hold

PUPILS ABOVE AVERAGE IN ENGLISH AND SCIENCE

School wins a good mark

ROLVENDEN county primary school has won good marks in an Ofs inspection report.

Barbara Scott, who took over as he teacher last spring, said the examinati was useful and she looks forward to bui ing on the many strengths identified.

The 89 pupils who are taught in four class were found to be above national averages English and Science.

Pupils with special educational needs we positive about their work and making soun progress.

The inspection team found good relationship between pupils and adults, with older pupils helping the younger.

The quality of teaching was sound overall, with detailed planning and clear learning objectives.

Mrs Scott provides good leadership and gives a clear educational direction for the work of the school.

The school is a secure, supportive carin ronment and the

Pupils go back to nature

THE ROYAL Mail community programme has sponsored a nature garden in the playground of Rolvenden primary school.

A patio has been provided, with bird table and plants and shrubs to attract butterflies.

The request for sponsorship came via Rolvenden area postman Graham Button, the

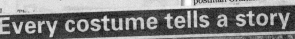

Every costume tells a story

...picting ...d ...the day ...ry

was transformed into the Lady of Shallot, while secretary Sue Clout was busy at work in the guise of Wee Willie Winkie.

Teacher Maralyn Button ar-

ety of characters, including Queen of Hearts, Little Bo Peep, Incy Wincy Spider, Tweedle Dum and Tweedle Dee, Fred and Barney Flintstone and Minny Ha Ha.

"The week has gone very well, ...have thoroughly

HERE'S HOW IT'S DONE: Pupils from Julie Burvill's class 4 demonstr mation-technology skills

Youngsters put poetry on parade

PUPILS at Rolvenden Primary School are well-versed in poetry after a workshop and readings by writer and storyteller John Rice.

The school held a poetry week and a parade in costumes of their favourite literary characters.

Youth and community librarian Kate Pariain, also spoke on the poetry theme, at the invitation of head teacher Barbara Scott.

The week's activities were co-ordinated by English teacher Maralyn Button.

John Rice lives in Cranbrook and writes for adults and children.

POPULAR VISITOR: John Rice with some of the pupils he entertained at Rolvenden

IT'S SIMPLE: Teacher Julie Burvill gives an IT lesson to parents   9A/0727E

Parents find surfing easy

...NY parents surfed the ...rnet for the first time in ...r lives when they attended ...information ...munication Technology ...evening at Rolvenden ...ary school.

...children showed them ...t was done, as well as ...a scanner for a word

processing programme, a digital camera displaying instant pictures, and a laptop among their eight computers.

Headteacher Barbara Scott said the children used ICT for all subjects and have been inspired by the National Grid for Learning projects. From the reception class upwards,

they learn keyboard skills.

The chairman of the governors Jan Stickland and others were impressed by their enthusiasm. The wildlife section on the Internet has become a favourite with pupils, who have been using it to watch animals at a waterhole in Africa.

PE equipment. The Post Office also donated plants and paving stones to surround the pond in the nature garden. In return the school kept its facilities open as far as possible for village use: the photocopier was open to all for a donation, as it had been for many years, and lamination was also offered. When the Church Room was being demolished and rebuilt to a newly-designed Village Hall in 2000, the school hall was offered for use by those organisations who found themselves without a venue in which to meet.

Judy Burvill left the same year and was given a send-off befitting her long association with Rolvenden, complete with another Sue Clout cake. She went on to become an ICT trainer for the Kent Advisory Service, having gained a taste for the subject at Rolvenden, and thus became a frequent return visitor. It was therefore appropriate that later that year the school's internet connection was upgraded to ISBN for the first time: a further nod to the new world of information into which the pupils were passing. With faster capabilities the Web started to become more of a teaching tool than simply a means of communication, and it began to find its way into every classroom. There was perhaps no more apt marker for the end of an extraordinary century in which the school had already progressed so much.

Chapter 10

INTO THE FUTURE

2001-21

THE DAWNING OF the new millennium saw further sad goodbyes as the school bid farewell first to Mrs Taylor, who took early retirement after 25 years; Anita Bond, headed for a deputy headship in East Sussex; and caretaker Norma Booker, who resigned due to ill health. Within a few months replacements had been found and a new era kicked off with the following teaching staff in harness: Maralyn Button and Brigitte McKinlay in the Reception class, and Diana Carter and Jane Doyle with the older infants; Janet Andrews in Class 3 and Gill Johnson with Mrs Smith and Mrs Petry in Class 4. Tracey Brooks took over as cleaner, Michelle Warnes in the kitchen, and later on that year Mrs Bowles took a well-earned retirement from teaching the piano. In 2002 Miss Carter gave way to newly-qualified teacher Ellen Jones, and Mrs Andrews to Janet May. Dick Dyer – son-in-law of Bessie Elliott – took over the role of maintaining the swimming pool which grew to general caretaker and handyman, and after a year he started as a classroom assistant alongside Miss Jones; later joined in the same role by Julie Hodgkins.

The four classes in 2001.

These were years of measurable success, evidenced by a slew of awards: two 'Quality Marks' awarded by the Basic Skills Agency, reflecting efforts to raise standards in English and mathematics; an 'Investor in People' award for good practice in training and development; a 'School Achievement Award' recognising the contribution of all the staff towards pupil attainment. Then, insofar as such things are important, the Autumn 2002 performance tables placed Rolvenden School within the top 25 in the county. It was part of this rigorous drive towards excellence that encouraged Mrs Scott to run an after-school Latin club for several years, on the premise that the inherent logic of the ancient language would better help pupils to understand English grammar.

The school received an 'Investor in People' award in 2002.

Sports, too, reached heights not seen for many years; despite the disruption of foot-and-mouth disease in 2001, the football and netball teams managed to keep their momentum going to the point that, in the following season, every single fixture was won. The netballers also won their Weald of Kent Schools Sports tournament, and the footballers were only runners-up due to goal difference; though, as ever, Mrs Scott was most delighted that 'both teams displayed good sportsmanship on and off the pitch.'

Even stronger links were forged with the wider community, particularly the church, whose members began to attend and contribute to assemblies in a greater capacity than previously. Improvements to the school fabric were funded with contributions from the Basil Russell Trust, Korker's Sausages and several other local businesses. The PTA took on a new lease of life, rebranding itself as the Friends of Rolvenden School to better suggest the inclusion of ex-pupils and teachers, non-teaching staff and community-minded helpers. Its major fundraising drive in these years was for improvements to the pool – something of a continuing theme – including a heating system and new cover. Two parents, Georgina Lowe and Michele Bradshaw, undertook a sponsored swim of the Tenterden Leisure Centre pool which raised over £300, and a Christmas Fayre took nearly £900 towards the cause. The school community was also humbled and gratified to receive generous legacies for school causes from the estates of Norma Booker and Harry Millum.

The highly-anticipated residential trips settled into a regular pattern, with trips to Marchant's Hill in Surrey alternating with those to Hardelot in northern France; thus every pupil in the top two years had the opportunity to attend at least one or both. The French visits were more cultural, with visits to a chocolatier, fromagerie, Boulogne market and the cemeteries of the First World War; while Marchant's Hill allowed the children to enjoy abseiling, climbing, rifle shooting, archery, fencing, hiking, quad biking and a zip wire. The staff and helpers who gamely accompanied the children on these trips were also compelled to join in, often with unintentionally

Scenes from the Marchant's Hill residential trips.

hilarious consequences. The same spirit was in the air back at Rolvenden and led to the installation of a new adventure playground in 2004, though this time the staff – mostly – were able to resist joining in.

Cathy Dalton, a teacher with much experience both abroad and in the UK, began in 2003, and the following year Mrs Button retired after 22 years taking care of the youngest pupils and was afforded the traditional warm send-off. Her strong links to the school would not be cast off entirely, and she remained active in the FORS association, taking joint charge with husband Graham of the always-memorable annual quiz. In her place came one of her ex-pupils, Esme King – soon to be Mrs Thomas – who had enjoyed previous careers in publishing and marketing and was appointed by Mrs Scott on a fast-track graduate teaching scheme. She enjoyed long-lasting family links with the school and its staff, being the granddaughter of Joan Edmonds, great-niece of Angela Edmonds, niece of Judy Burvill and daughter of Jackie King who had founded the Rolvenden Preschool in 1982.

Changes to educational practices were in the air, leading – inevitably – to an increased workload. In 2005 the school welcomed Liz Barrett, initially as a part-time support to allow teachers some dedicated time for preparation, planning and assessment. Mrs Barrett later went on to teach science and religious education across the school, and regular supply teacher Frances Trumper offered additional assistance. Pupil numbers were now healthy enough for a fifth class was opened up in the school hall. This meant that the village hall was hired for two afternoons a week for the PE sessions – with the unfortunate leakage of exuberant noise into the serenity of a neighbouring yoga class. It was something of a relief when permission was granted for a new mobile classroom to be installed on the school site, and both school and village halls were was freed up once more.

Technology had moved on greatly since the first, tentative steps in computing some 20 years before, and 2005 saw the installation of a state-of-the-art interactive whiteboard in each classroom. Good practice with regard to using the Internet became a feature of all subjects on the curriculum; and soon Mrs Thomas was requesting village correspondents to email her so that the pupils could formulate their replies. The staff was replenished again the following year by the arrival of Abi Cottrell and learning support assistant Lisa Bloomsmar.

To any outside observer of the school, one of the most remarkable themes of the next few years was the ambition and scale of some of the school productions, at which the wider community were warmly invited to attend. Miss Jones and Mrs Thomas were the driving force behind these shows which would grow to magnificent proportions. An early example was *The Wish Factory*, which was formed out of ideas gathered in a workshop run by the Royal Opera House which both teachers attended in 2006. They returned to the school with the idea of encouraging their pupils to write, compose, act and perform their own opera which, in the manner of Glyndebourne, was presented over two summer nights on the school field after a picnic supper. There cannot be many primary schools to have worked in the opera genre, still less with the youngest pupils; when one considers that the whole production was devised by the children themselves, the achievement is astonishing.

After ten years at Rolvenden, in 2006 Barbara Scott took the decision to move on. She was able to look back with much satisfaction, leaving a school with a good OFSTED rating and renewed vigour to build on its success. She wrote at the time:

> There have been many special occasions for me to treasure, but it is the day to day fun and comradeship that form the true foundation of my remembrances. I am leaving a truly remarkable place where every day brought something that we could smile about and some days brought unending joy! Whatever the future holds, I am sure that the spirit of this little school will live on and bring equal satisfaction to the new Headteacher.

Top marks for school

STAFF at Rolvenden Primary School know their pupils individually and encourage independent working.

This is the view of a team of Ofsted inspectors who paid a visit to the village school, which has a register of just under 100 pupils.

Staff were praised for the efforts they make to encourage personal development of the children and for how well they know their pupils.

Head teacher Barbara Scott said she was delighted that the hard work of the staff had been recognised. She said: "This is an encouraging report that endorsed the values that staff and governors hold dear. Creating the right learning environment is very important and we were pleased that the Ofsted inspectors took so much interest in this aspect of our school life."

The school is embarking on an exciting future with a project to create an interactive website and to upgrade the provision for the nursery.

THUMBS UP: Head Barbara Scott and Class 2 teacher Ellen Jones and her class celebrate their

Pupils enjoy fruits of their labour

STAFF at Rolvenden Primary School were busy serving up dinners and washing up the dishes in an effort to help children understand where food comes from.

Almost every child in the school was involved in the operation on Friday, which involved cooking dinner for all 107 pupils plus staff. And it went so well, staff say they want to do it again.

"The children seemed to thoroughly enjoy themselves and it went extremely well," said school secretary Sue Clout.

The event was organised to celebrate Harvest Festival. Parents were asked to donate basic ingredients so the children could whip up a three course meal.

They started with super vegetable soup, followed by crusty bread, chunky cheese and scrumptious salad, and finished with fruity crumble, creamy custard and bowls of fresh fruit salad.

"Every child had a chance to do something," added Mrs Clout. "We wanted to make the children appreciate how the food is grown, prepared and eaten.

"We are a farming community. It is surprising how many children do not appreciate where food comes from."

serving the food   Picture Gary Browne Ref: 446240

■ Natalie Rosie and Katherine in their Victorian outfits   Picture Dave Downey pd89Z397

Churches join for a Victorian sing-along

by Sarah Linney
slinney@thekmgroup.co.uk

VICTORIAN dress, songs and poems were brought into the present in Rolvenden on Saturday at a concert which raised more than £600 for good causes.

Around 150 people enjoyed singing, performances by harp, organ and guitar players and poetry readings in St Mary's Church.

Children from Rolvenden Primary School dressed in Victorian costumes to perform three songs from the musical Scrooge.

The evening was a joint venture with St Andrew's Catholic Church in Tenterden and half the money will go towards providing disabled access there.

The other half will help to pay for two-year-old Frank Guest, from Newenden, who has Down's Syndrome, to have one-to-one teaching at Rolvenden pre-school, which he attends.

WELL DONE: The Rolvenden girls who were winners of the Ashford Youth League Under-11 title with their awards presented at the league end of season tournament at Ball Lane in Ashford. Full story on page 86.   Ref:pd173896

Pupils make a little music

OLIVER! was the word in Rolvenden primary school when the Year 6 leavers put on a production of the musical.

Sue Clout, school secretary, said: "We had perfect weather and were able to perform in the playground.

"One hundred and eighty-five adults and children came along and they all enjoyed a buffet during the interval.

But it was the show itself that impressed most of all.

She added: "The pupils had been practising for weeks with their teacher Abbi Cotterill and learning support assistant Lisa Rivenmoor.

"We were able to obtain a grant towards costumes and sensory workshops.

"The audience enjoyed the evening and it was thanks for more and more."

PUPPET SHOW: Rolvenden Primary School pupils India Hoad, eight, and Olivia Lemon, nine, with the puppets they made

Postponed maypole dancing is chance to meet new head

■ Rolvenden school children dancing round the maypole

SCHOOLCHILDREN in Rolvenden put on an impressive display of maypole dancing at the village primary school last Friday.

The belated event – usually held on May 1, but postponed due to bad weather – also gave the pupils a chance to meet new head teacher Janet May, who starts in September and who taught at the school six years ago.

Acting head teacher Janet May, pictured, said: "Our school dates back to 1834 and the maypole dancing tradition here goes back 100 years.

"Friday's dance also gave the new head teacher a chance to meet parents."

She added: "The children love the dancing, it's one of the big highlights and Mrs Rivers had a lovely time and left a message on the board saying how friendly everyone was."

School camp

PARENTS and children from Rolvenden primary school enjoyed a camping trip in the playing field.

School secretary Sue Clout said: "The weather was perfect and 78 people brought their own tents.

"The event, which was organised by Janet May, our senior staff member and head of PE, included a barbecue and a game of rounders."

She added: "This was a special event which was just for fun - no fund-raising or cost involved. Everyone had a great time and there were cries of 'Can we camp again?' It may be an annual event."

Pupils say farewell to head teacher Barbara

ROLVENDEN'S school head teacher is leaving.

Barbara Scott is to leave in December after 10 years at the school and will work for Kent Advisory Service.

She said: "It is a really special school.

"The children are delightful, the parents are supportive and I have had a very good, hard working governing body. The school seems to attract staff who are dedicated and make my life so much easier."

Mrs Scott, who will continue to live in nearby Wittersham, will work around the county in an advisory capacity supporting schools across Kent.

She added: "It's going to be quite a challenge, but exciting.

Mrs Scott said that she would really miss the school and area. She said: "Rolvenden will be quite a wrench, it's a very special village, it's idyllic."

Janet May will be acting head teacher while the permanent replacement for Mrs Scott is sought.

Mrs Scott's new role was at the Kent Advisory Service, where part of her role was to step in to lead schools identified as being in difficulties. These experiences have made her appreciate the strengths of Rolvenden all the more, and she retains very fond memories of the decade she spent there.

While a new headteacher was sought Janet May stepped in with support from Chris Dale of Egerton School. The process took rather longer than everyone hoped, but by the summer of 2007 the right person had been found, and she was a familiar face. Since leaving for East Sussex six years previously Anita Bond had married John Rivers, and was thus justified in describing Rolvenden as 'a school very special to me personally and professionally.' Not only was the school redecorated and reorganised for her arrival but the ambience changed too: **Anita Rivers**' infectious laughter was soon to be frequently heard echoing up and down the corridors, and youthful exuberance was – if not encouraged, then certainly more than tolerated. During the summer months, it became a custom for pupils and staff alike to chant 'swim-ming, swim-ming' at excessive volume during breaks before a session in the pool.

Inspired by a visit to the school in Germany where her husband had previously taught, Mrs Rivers returned with the idea that a new, vibrant library with sensory aspects would be a real asset to the school. FORS and their chair, Nikki Payne, picked up the idea with untiring energy and called in several favours, amassing a group of parent helpers who willingly gave their time free of charge. Materials such as cupboards, shelves and flooring were supplied at cost price or at a considerable discount. The result – a library with the theme of 'Wonderland' – was a real success and truly unique. To celebrate its opening in June 2009 the poet Kit Wright spent a day in the school running creative workshops.

The opening of the new 'Wonderland' library in June 2009.

Shortly afterwards Sue Clout resigned as secretary after 22 years at the helm; giving way to Sandy Hughes. But Mrs Clout did not leave altogether: she remained in the new part-time role of Family Liaison Officer, strengthening a vital link between school and community, and held a useful Friday café in the new library for several years. New arrivals at this time were teaching assistants Laura Dullar and Christopher Rivers, son of ex-headteacher John.

Ambition and colour were the watchwords to many school activities. The successful production duo of Jones and Thomas scored more hits with outdoor performances of *A Midsummer Night's Dream*, *Romeo and Juliet* (both largely to Shakespeare's original text) and *Robin Hood* – for all of which the whole school was invited to audition, and parts found for all willing participants. A new mini orchard was planted and outside classroom made of green oak installed in 2010, and on the initiative of Mrs Barrett, the school was awarded a Green Flag, the highest distinction of an 'Eco School.' Furthermore, the pupils were already recognised as 'High Weald Heroes,' having gained an understanding as to how the historical practices of pannage and droving had shaped the environment in which they lived and worked.

All these efforts notwithstanding, by 2011 it was clear something was missing. Rolvenden School was acknowledged by everyone who knew it to be a friendly, caring and happy place, with staff full of energy and enthusiasm, and facilities that were both first-rate in quality and entirely suited to its environment as a rural village school. Yet these qualities seemed to pass by both the education officials and prospective parents and, since the peak school roll in 2004, places were now not being filled as one might have expected – when Mrs Cottrell left, it reverted back to a three-class school once more. In short, what was clear to insiders was not as obvious to many outside of Rolvenden: the school was guilty of hiding its light under a bushel.

A FORS meeting identified that a major public relations exercise was needed to alter the perception of the school, and it was decided that a large-scale event with wide attendance would display its key qualities to the best advantage. It was suggested that the school take on the mantle of the village fete which Rolvenden no longer held: thus the annual Woodland Day was born, held for the first time in June 2011. A heartfelt appeal for help in different woodcraft and associated activities enjoyed a huge response: it was later estimated that around 85% of the parent body helped with the first event – where previously, as with parent-teacher associations the world over, the same few people tended to do all the work. Thousands of promotional leaflets were printed and distributed with the *Wealden Advertiser*. The practice of charging an entrance fee which gave access to all activities was also a bold innovation. Both in terms of its short- and long-term goals, Rolvenden's Woodland Day was an immediate and resounding success, and there is anecdotal evidence to suggest that several families were impressed enough to send their children to Rolvenden despite living some distance away.

The template of the Woodland Day was lifted wholesale for the first Winter Wonderland event six months later, replacing the Christmas Fayre which had become rather lacklustre. This immediately matched the success of the summer event, and within a couple of years was offering diversions and activities of an astonishing range:

> Candle dipping, lavender bag making, edible reindeer, creating gingerbread and marzipan penguins, angel decorating, conker-necklace stringing, bulb planting, wooden reindeer and snowman constructing, damper bread and marshmallow cooking, drumming workshop, seasonal science activities, Christmas market.

Scenes from the Woodland Day events.

With a decade's service at Rolvenden under her belt, Mrs May left for Cranbrook in 2012, and her place was filled by Mike Dixon from Sussex, previously a headteacher for 20 years, who shared the class duties with Mrs Barrett. This arrangement was supposed to last two terms, but Mr Dixon was happily prevailed upon to stay for more than three years. Mrs Dullar also moved away and in successive years Roisin Golan and Emily Jones – known as 'Miss J' to avoid confusion with Ellen Jones – were welcomed into the fold as teaching assistants. The school hall was opened up to a '2 o'clock club' for toddlers run by the SureStart Centre each Thursday which offered messy play, active movement and art and craft.

Oliver!, performed at Smallhythe Place, 2012.

In 2012 Miss Jones and Mrs Thomas were exploring even more ambitious avenues for the school productions. They had remained in contact with Cathy Dalton, now volunteering at Smallhythe Place, and it was suggested that they could stage a performance of the musical *Oliver!* in the historic Barn Theatre, to tie in with a whole-school Victorian theme. Susannah Mayor, the curator, coached the young actors in diction and projection, and acted as liaison with the National Trust – as it was to be the first ever amateur school production performed there. A marquee was erected as the 'green room' and the production ran over three nights in March, with Mrs Button brought back to provide piano accompaniment. Because of the fact that a West End production was running concurrently, Rolvenden's cast also had to perform the full version – no allowances were made for the fact that the performers were of school age.

The Young Voices Choir at the O$_2$ Arena.

The church continued to reach out to the school and, in a joint venture between staff and church volunteers, a breakfast club was started offering cereals, toast and fruit juice before school one morning each week. Soon it was inviting pupils to attend by offering five free places per week, chosen on a rota system through the register, and within a year the take-up had trebled. Church workers from both Rolvenden and Wittersham also visited the school once a month as part of the 'Open the Book' initiative, re-enacting Bible stories with costumes and props. The children also had the opportunity to perform at the O$_2$ Arena when parent and road crossing patrolman Neil Cackett began a Young Voices Choir and a smaller School Choir. This much-anticipated event continues to this day.

Horizons were broadened further with regular use of the facilities at Benenden Girls' School as part of their community outreach programme. Outside interests and extra-curricular activities blossomed to the extent that no pupil could say they were not offered something to tempt them. Take this list from 2013:

> *football; netball; tennis; speed, agility and quickness; dance and fitness; ecology; art; science; flower club; table top games; gardening; cooking; LEGO; choir.*

Even more ambition was to be seen in the same year's Smallhythe production and, once again, it was to break new ground. Miss Jones and Mrs Thomas's first attempt to produce *The Lion King* had been rebuffed by Disney but, undaunted, they kept trying. Eventually the world's biggest multinational media and entertainment conglomerate conceded that yes, they were looking into producing a 'schools' version of the musical, and perhaps Rolvenden's production might be the pilot? Thus it was that over several nights in June 2013 the pupils put on a musical on a scale they had never attempted before, to an enraptured audience of parents, friends, and several Disney executives. They were impressed enough to pave the way for other similar musicals to be produced in subsequent years, such as *The Jungle Book*, *The Little Mermaid* and *Aladdin*.

Smallhythe Place performances were generally repeated on the school field.

Above and below, pupils from Rolvenden Primary School who dressed up and took part in activities for a Dickens day

Pupils' education given a little Twist!

PUPILS at Rolvenden Primary School stopped back in time for a Victorian day.

Those in key stage 2 studied Charles Dickens

predecessors would have done, such as technical drawing, drill, art and drama.

The day was part of a Victorian project, which ends in a whole school production

fundraising
day centre

Schoolchildren are in tune with nature

ABOUT 30 children and parents from Rolvenden primary school enjoyed an early start to their day recently when they took part in a Birdsong and Breakfast event.

Teacher Esme Thomas said: "Local bird enthusiast Charles Trollope offered to come to the school early one morning to help us identify birds and their songs.

"We met at 8am, with our binoculars, on the school field and watched and listened.

"We spent just over half an hour walking around our field and the one next to it and heard a robin, a chaffinch, a black cap, a great tit, a blackbird, a wood pigeon, a wren and many more."

She added: "Then we all went into the school hall for a delicious breakfast that had been organised by Friends of Rolvenden School.

"Everybody really enjoyed it and learned a lot and we hope to make it an annual event."

School full of outlaws!

ROBIN Hood came to Rolvenden when pupils at the primary school staged a popular outdoor production about the outlaw of Sherwood Forest.

Hood himself, pupil George Benson, even received a message of good luck from the actor playing the role in the BBC production, Jonah Armstrong.

Teacher Esme Thomas said: "It was fantastic - very well supported, a lovely evening and everyone remembered their lines."

The school's field and its many trees made an ideal Sherwood Forest. All the costumes were supplied by Bodiam Castle.

Ms Thomas added: "Afterwards we had up to 91 families camping in the field."

Medieval maidens at Rolvenden PD1597177

Robin Hood, played by George Benson
Picture: Gary Browne

Learning to be like Egyptians

PUPILS at Rolvenden Primary School took a step back in time to mark the 89th anniversary of the re-discovery of Tutankhamun's tomb.

Children from Years 3 and 4 dressed up as Egyptians to commemorate the discovery of the young pharaoh by archaeologist Howard Carter in November 1922.

The pupils from Willow Class, who have been learning about the Ancient Egyptians, dressed up in costumes, played games and took part in creative activities on Friday, November 4.

Tutankhamun, who was King of Egypt from 1336 until 1327BC, died aged 18 and was buried in a hastily prepared tomb in the Valley of the Kings at Thebes, Egypt.

Mr Carter, on an expedition funded by Lord Carnarvon, started digging on November 1, eventually discovering the first flight of stairs down into the tomb on November 4.

It was the most intact tomb ever discovered and contained so many artifacts it took a decade just to catalogue them.

school of the week

Small but with a big heart

By Emma Seymour

SITUATED in a rural vi Rolvenden Primary is but privileged, with facilities than an av school.

Based at the same site it was founded in the 186 40 pupils at the Hasting school have the advanta heated swimming p sports field and an ad playground.

Classrooms still sit original building, altho the 1980s two blocks, to once have been u arately for boys and gi linked.

Work is continuing the present day, as th activity area 'is being revamped in project.

The space, mainly quiet work such a crafts, is being fres ated and renovated more storage space.

An outdoor class was also recently for the foundation way of a creative in which a profes worked with childr the space.

Foundation cla Ellen Jones said: children helped willow tunnel an enjoyed that.

"It was nice fo something for so to appreciate."

There are a nu and extra-curri ies offered to pu ferent options

each term, including football, netball, construction, art, choir and gardening.

IN CHARGE: Headteacher Anita Rivers

Fred Butler-Graham makes his den FM265342

Pupils put their eco enemies under fire

DEN building and paintball firing at less than eco-friendly targets were among attractions at a woodland day at Rolvenden Primary School.

The school's field hosted a range of activities for the family day out on Saturday.

Teacher and organiser Esme Thomas said it was an opportunity to showcase their eco-credentials.

She said: "We are an eco school and came up with the idea last year for a fun family day which promotes our eco work.

"This year more than 200 children completed activity cards which is double the number last year."

Families paid £5 admission for activities which included making fire, wearing camouflage to stalk through long grass, building a den, woodwork, nature walks and paintballing at static targets representing global warming and pollution.

Mrs Thomas said that families attended from further afield as well as school pupils.

"It is not a money-making event," she added. "It is affordable for all."

This team pull together to build their den at Rolvenden Primary School
Picture: Paul Amos FM265346

Left, camouflaged and ready to enter into the woodland fun, Amie Gregory, Danielle Egglesden and Harvey Egglesden FM265392

Hannah Fleming ties some branches to cover her den FM265391

Education Secretary Michael Gove's reforms to the National Curriculum, which began a hurried implementation in September 2014, caused a degree of turmoil that is still being felt in the education sector. To those teachers who had themselves been taught according to the 'old' National Curriculum, the changes were largely seen as overly prescriptive and inflexible, reducing schooling to a soulless box-ticking exercise. This, of course, was quite at odds with Rolvenden's ethos of catering for the whole child, and it is no wonder that many staff here – as with those in the profession more widely – began to feel dispirited by the so-called 'progress.' At the very least, it caused yet another readjustment to practices with which people had felt secure.

Troubles never come on their own, so they say. The upheaval of the new curriculum in 2014 coincided with a cancer diagnosis for Mrs Rivers; she was compelled to take time off and Emma Dyer, of Bethersden, was brought in as acting headteacher. It was a testing time for all: the inevitable disruption of a new regime mingled with a lot of personal worry about Mrs Rivers' situation, and nobody had any idea how longstanding the arrangement would turn out to be. Happily, Mrs Rivers responded to treatment and was well enough to return to Rolvenden; however, she rightly decided that the stresses of a school environment would not be conducive to her healing, and she resigned as headteacher in October 2015. It was clearly the correct decision: now fully recovered, she lives in New Romney with John Rivers and enjoys a new career in retail sales.

Yet within this maelstrom could always be found reasons to be cheerful. Pupil numbers had recovered sufficiently for a fourth class to be reopened in the mobile, and Lucy Gillespie-Tomasevic was appointed to take it. Shortly afterwards came teaching assistant Mrs Anderson-Frogley and Ms Springell as part-time Family Liaison Officer. The centenary of the First World War engaged the pupils in a village-wide commemoration, and Jackie King's researches into those who died helped them to appreciate the sacrifices made by those not so much older than themselves. The swimming pool was again out of service but FORS were able to confound the naysayers who suggested it be mothballed by raising several thousands in a very short time to get it up and running again. The profits of a successful Woodland Day (the fifth) helped, as did a Dragon Race at Bewl Water at which Rolvenden's team placed eleventh out of 67.

Sarah O'Neill before her appointment to Rolvenden.

Mr Dixon and Mrs Gillespie-Tomasevic left in 2015 and were replaced by Alexandra Shorter and Sophie Lorimore, and Hannah Whitlock joined shortly afterwards to take years 1 and 2. There was finally news on a new headteacher as well: she was 35-year-old **Sarah O'Neill**, born in Southampton, raised in Cornwall and then Kent. She graduated from Canterbury Christ Church College and gained a wide teaching experience from several primary schools in the county: Snodland CE, Eastborough in Maidstone; Mundella in Folkestone.

Mrs O'Neill was everybody's friend, and her calm professionalism and organisational skills helped to stabilise the running of a school that had been in a state of flux for some time – to which the good 2017 OFSTED report made reference. She appreciated straightaway what made Rolvenden 'tick,' and her values aligned with those of the rest of the staff, parents and pupils. She was also open with the fact that she had previously survived a bout of cancer in 2012-3, and therefore knew intimately the challenges to be faced in that respect. The pupils loved her humanity and the kindliness of her nature. It was Mrs O'Neill who introduced the six CREATE values which endure at Rolvenden still: creativity, resilience, engagement, aspiration, teamwork and enjoyment.

After a year of strong performances all round, in September 2017 Mrs O'Neill was diagnosed with secondary breast cancer and admitted to the Pilgrims' Hospice. James Tibbles of Phoenix Primary School in Ashford was brought in as part-time acting headteacher: history was surely repeating itself. For a year her friends and colleagues watched anxiously the pace of her recovery, and the pupils were also kept informed as far as was appropriate. Mrs O'Neill returned to the school on a part-time basis in October 2018 to an outpouring of affection and not a little relief, and spent a good deal of energy remodelling the school for greater efficiency. The library and mobile classroom were swapped around, and the nature garden refreshed. The pupils were present and visible at the commemorations of the ending of the First World War in November 2018. Staff members contributed to a push on team sports, with much success: the football team won the Weald of Kent Schools Sports tournament, and teams were fielded in further competitions for netball, cross-country and even a swimming gala.

Sarah O'Neill, 1980-2020.

Very sadly, Mrs O'Neill's recovery was to be short-lived. As her health deteriorated once more she took early retirement and left the school in July 2019. It was a time of regret and much sadness all round, which also coincided with the departures of Mrs Thomas, Miss Jones, Mrs Barrett and Miss Storr. Sarah O'Neill returned to the Pilgrims' Hospice for palliative care, remaining cheerful and resolute throughout her dreadful ordeal. She died in January 2020, aged 39, and was brought back to Rolvenden for burial as she had wished. She now rests in the churchyard, wrapped in the patchwork blanket to which each of her pupils contributed a square, a stone's throw from the school that she loved and which – if it were possible – loved her even more in return.

To **Nick Leggat** fell the task of rejuvenating a school buffeted by a time of instability and now stunned by loss. Raised in south Wales, Mr Leggat had trained at Canterbury Christ Church College and worked at various schools in the Ashford area – Kingsnorth, Kennington and Oak Tree – before spending twelve years as Deputy Head at Tenterden CE Junior School. It was here that links with Rolvenden began to be established, when Executive Headteacher Sam Crinnion stepped in for a period during Mrs O'Neill's absence in September 2018, effectively sharing the role for the rest of that academic year. Mr Leggat began his post as interim Headteacher at Rolvenden in September 2019, joined by his Tenterden colleague Ben Vincer as Deputy Head.

For some years up to this point, extensive discussion had taken place on securing the future of the school. Its continued survival was by no means a given: small schools are expensive to run and, thanks to the wide fluctuation in numbers year-on-year, are often unpredictable to budget for. As has been seen throughout its history, Rolvenden has suffered more than most from lack of investment by the education authorities. One idea was to convert the school to an academy, which was a growing nationwide movement and – at the time – encouraged by central government. Effectively the school would no longer be run by Kent's LEA but would take greater control of its finances, staffing and management through a new academy trust, either on its own or through a shared trust with other schools. Pluckley and Smarden Schools (in federation) had recently joined the Kemnal Trust, running over forty schools in the south-east, but it was felt that too much of Rolvenden's character might be lost if aligned to such a large organisation.

A possible solution presented itself from December 2016, when the Tenterden Schools Trust – consisting of Homewood, Tenterden Primary Federation, St Michaels School and Home Farm Nursery – was formed. The school governors approached the Trust as part of a consultation programme lasting through 2017-18. Here seemed a far better fit for Rolvenden: locally-based, freer access to suppliers, a dedicated maintenance team pooled across relatively few schools, impressive shared resources and stronger links with Homewood, to where the majority of Rolvenden's leavers go. The governors gave their approval; and while the transfer only happened after her tenure had ended, in November 2019, Mrs O'Neill's enthusiasm – together with the established staffing links with Tenterden – was a major factor in winning hearts and minds, and achieving a smooth transition.

The school became an academy under the Tenterden Schools Trust in November 2019.

Rolvenden now part of town schools trust

Tiny village school becomes academy

by Rachael Woods
rwoods@thekmgroup.co.uk

Rolvenden Primary School has become an academy and is now part of the Tenterden Schools Trust.

Its conversion follows a successful consultation with governors, staff and parents at the school, which was previously rated 'good' by Ofsted.

Samantha Crinnion, who is in charge of the Tenterden Primary Federation, has become executive head teacher at Rolvenden, while Nick Leggat remains as head of school.

The tiny school, founded in 1827, has just over 100 pupils and officially joined the trust on November 1.

Tenterden Schools Trust was launched in December 2016 to unite four Tenterden schools under a multi-academy trust consisting of Homewood School

Tenterden Schools Trust chief executive Sally Lees

& Sixth Form Centre with Home Farm Nursery, Tenterden infant and junior schools (Tenterden Primary Federation) and St Michaels primary.

Tenterden Schools Trust chief executive Sally Lees said: "We are absolutely delighted to welcome Rolvenden Primary School to our trust.

"We have been working closely with the school over the last year and it is so pleasing to be able to confirm that our close relationship will continue into the future.

"Rolvenden is a small village school dedicated to serving its local community.

"We are confident that Rolvenden will be able to continue to provide an excellent education to current and future cohorts of children."

One of the first joint projects to be undertaken saw children from Rolvenden and Tenterden juniors working together to create a Christmas market installation in front of St Mildred's church made from more than 1,400 recycled bottles.

Rolvenden Primary School – as it now is, relieved of its 'County School' status – stands today as the epitome of a small, rural village school with a fine and rich history. Ask anyone who has been associated with the school what is so special about it, and their responses always include the same word: 'family.' This is both a reflection of the caring nature of staff-pupil and inter-pupil relationships, and the fact that its place in the community has been assured by generations of the same family – five or six generations, in some cases – who continue to attend what they are proud to call 'their school.' Nick Leggat has his own view:

> *Although all families have their disagreements and fallings-out they also have that love for all the members, large and small, and the desire for those members to have the best experiences in life. That's what Rolvenden, in association with the TST, is about: providing the core learning to ensure the brightest futures for its children, developing its staff professionally to enhance current and future careers choices whilst endeavouring to enrich the school experience of everyone lucky enough to be involved with the school as far as is humanly possible.*

If the timing is right, a visitor to the school may cross the road with the assistance of Mrs Gregory who also works as a midday supervisor and, as the granddaughter of Avril Bryant, is continuing something of a family tradition. He will walk down the north drive to the rear gate, perhaps musing that the mobile classroom next to the staff car park was once the site of a rusting piece of war detritus that stood for over thirty years. Then the screening of the field from the school buildings is down to the row of oak trees planted by Mr Spelling's pupils in the 1970s. He is buzzed in at the gate by either Mrs Hughes or Mrs Catt – security is paramount, but not at the expense of pleasantness. The clerical staff – supported by Ms Wellstead, who is also the kitchen manager – and Mr Leggat occupy the offices built in 1989 for their use. Though based in Tenterden, Ms Crinnion remains Executive Headteacher of both Rolvenden and the Tenterden Primary Federation, and has a regular on-site presence.

Reception pupils begin in Hazel Class with Mr Heath, supported by Mrs Dowdeswell and Miss Milton, based appropriately in the original 1877 infants' schoolroom. They then proceed to another room of the 1989 extension for Oak Class with Miss Whitlock in years 1 and 2, with assistance from Miss Jones, Mrs Charlton and Mrs Kaczmarek. Willow Class comes next for years 3 and 4: Mr Leader, with Mrs Anderson-Frogley and Mrs Antrum, in the 1912 classroom. The upper two years in Holly Class are taught jointly by Mr Vincer, Mr Leggat and Mrs Crowe, supported by Mrs Golan and Mrs Reynolds, in a mobile classroom on the playground – for the time being, at least.

In October 2020 the Tenterden Schools Trust was successful in obtaining planning permission for the school's fourth major extension in its history. The mobile classroom and air-raid shelter will go, and the reception area will be extended outwards and modernised to include a new office, with the old one converted to a meeting room. Two spacious modern classrooms will be accessed through a corridor to the north-west, passing by a modern lavatory suite which will alleviate some of the many problems experienced with the old ones over the years – which still stand on the original Victorian site, despite refurbishments. At time of writing funding for the work is being sought, but this future development should resolve most of the overcrowding and fabric issues that have dogged the school more or less since the building opened in 1837.

If only all problems were as predictable and solvable. The Covid-19 pandemic of 2020-1 has cut a swathe through society in general, and though the continuing provision of education has been rightly prioritised, schools have experienced a level of disruption not seen since the Second World War. In Rolvenden's case, the association with the Tenterden Schools Trust came as a truly fortuitous piece of good timing. During the first national school closure from March to July 2020, the children of key workers attended lessons in the more spacious surroundings of Homewood School, where a 'Hub School' had been set up within two days of the lockdown being announced. Those who remained at home were set tasks remotely over the Internet and communications established through ClassDojo. On the resumption of classes at the school in September 2020, challenges relating to social distancing in the essentially Victorian building were overcome, and the provision of

hand sanitizer and common-sense approach to wearing masks at drop-off and pick-up times helped to alleviate the natural anxiety of parents, pupils and staff. The summer and Christmas plays even went ahead; filmed for posterity and streamed for home viewing. During the second closure from January to March 2021 lessons were given to pupils at home in a mix of pre-recorded and live formats, and virtual 'attendance' at these remained remarkably high. Mr Leggat comments:

> *In spite of some horror stories from schools around the country, where staff and parents were highly stressed, the Rolvenden community, through good communication all round, have seemed incredibly relaxed, yet vigilant, in the face of the threat of the virus. This is to the credit of all families and staff who have been in close communication with the school.*

A visitor to any school today will not see it as it ought to be; with one-way systems, chalked arrows and taped-off areas bearing unhappy testimony. We in 2021 are in the midst of a moment in time that will eventually pass. But when it does, the community of the little school at Rolvenden will be able to both look back in satisfaction that it did what was proper and right, and forward to greater and more lasting glories to come; in the knowledge that their work is valued and their position secure, and as befits a school with at least three hundred years of history behind it.

This, then, is the story of Rolvenden School: a small school at the centre of its village which, for over three centuries now, has made a big difference and continues to do so.